DON'T CLOSE THE DOOR!

DON'T CLOSE THE DOOR!

Winning and Keeping the Cultist for Christ

DOUG HARRIS

REACHOUT TRUST
Morden, England

ISBN 0 9513632 0 0

Scripture quotations are from the NASB © The Lockman
Foundation 1960, 1962, 1963, 1968, 1971, 1972, 1973, 1975, 1977.
Used by permission. Other versions used—NIV & NWT (New
World Translation).

Production and Printing in England for
REACHOUT TRUST
Alpha Place, Garth Road, Morden, Surrey SM4 4LX by
Nuprint Ltd, Station Road, Harpenden, Herts AL5 4SE

DEDICATION

My sincere thanks to the different people who have given willingly of their time to share with me, and now with us all, their life stories.

My thanks also to the many helpers in the Reachout Team who make the work possible.

Finally, and especially, my thanks to my wife Noemi and children Joel, Debbie and Luke who put up with their dad being away so much.

CONTENTS

Introduction *Doug Harris* — 9

Truth Made Me Leave Jehovah's Witnesses
Philip Mawson — 11

Trying To Be A Worthy Mormon *Brian Rendell* — 25

Obedient To Jehovah's Organization *Jean Norris* — 35

From Joseph Smith To Jesus Christ *Ann Thomas* — 43

Thirty-one Years A Jehovah's Witness *Jean Cleave* — 55

One Of The Great Crowd Of Jehovah's Witnesses
Robert Stewart — 65

Jehovah's Witnesses, Revelation And The Great
Crowd *Robert Stewart* — 73

Winning And Keeping The Cultist For Christ
Doug Harris — 99

Glossary Of Jehovah's Witness Terms — 107

Glossary Of Mormon Terms — 111

INTRODUCTION

Many people have asked us for the testimonies of ex-Jehovah's Witnesses and ex-Mormons and at last we have put together this short book. The testimonies included here may not all be very dramatic but each one of them is a glorious triumph for the Lord Jesus.

All of these people were genuine adherents when they were involved in the cults. They really believed their particular cult was true and at first they had no need to look elsewhere. It was only as a result of the work of the Holy Spirit, either directly through the Word of God or, more often, through a Christian, that they had the opportunity to find the real Jesus.

The purpose of this book is to encourage every Christian to understand that talking to the Mormon or Witness at your door is really worthwhile. As we have taken seminars in churches all over Britain we have heard many excuses as to why we should not talk to these people. One of the most common is, 'It's not worth talking to them, they've made up their minds already!' This book should put pay to that excuse once and for all.

Other excuses we hear include 'I'm fearful of getting involved' and 'I don't know enough about my own doctrines to talk with them.' To a certain extent these two excuses will be answered by this book but you will find other helpful literature on the resource list of Reachout

Trust, Alpha Place, Garth Road, Morden, Surrey SM4 4LX (081-337 9716). Make contact if we can be of any further help to you.

Be encouraged—the caller at your door is genuine. At some point in his life he has reached out for God and sadly been misled. At the doorstep you have the tremendous privilege of sharing the real Jesus and the way of salvation with him. Do get yourself prepared so you don't miss the next opportunity.

If you have difficulty in understanding any of the terms used in the various testimonies, turn to the glossary of unfamiliar terms at the end of the book.

To any Jehovah's Witness or Mormon who reads this book we also extend the invitation to contact us as we would love to arrange for someone to help you further. Our desire is not just to get you out of one organization and into another but to introduce you to the real Jesus of Scripture who we know you have a longing to meet.

Please make sure you also see the video that goes with this book. There you will meet many of the people in this book face to face. You will see the genuineness of their struggle to find the truth and the peace and rest that they have now entered into.

Finally, we want you to know that we are available to help and support you in any way we can so that you *Don't Close The Door.*

Doug Harris
Reachout Trust
November 1990

Truth Made Me Leave Jehovah's Witnesses

Philip Mawson

I began to study with Jehovah's Witnesses in 1979, and after just six months of their indoctrination I was baptized and so began my time of whole-souled devotion to the Watchtower Society. I continued with zeal and dedication until early 1989 when my devotion and loyalty to the Watchtower organization was shattered beyond repair. Watchtower doctrine and Bible truth clashed head on! I found myself faced with the biggest decision of my life, and in the cause of truth and for the love of God, I disassociated myself from the Watchtower organization.

Joining the ranks of Jehovah's Witnesses was quite simple, even exciting—much like the proverbial 'fly in the jam pot'—but getting out was a very different matter. I found myself in a very sticky situation that had a traumatic effect on me emotionally, mentally and spiritually. But, praise Jesus, I am now free from Watchtower chains, born again in the Spirit of God. Not only that—my mother, brother-in-law, younger brother and another person associated with the Jehovah's Witnesses also accompanied me in my exodus from the organization.

As I share my experience I hope that it will promote understanding and consolation, particularly so if you are, at this moment, one of Jehovah's Witnesses whose conscience is troubled by the incompatibility of 'Watchtowerism' and Bible truth. This realization is admittedly

11

devastating at first, especially when the full impact of it hits you. I know because when I actually found out that what was supposed to be God's organization—the organization which controlled my thinking and actions for ten years—was nothing but one of the many cults that counterfeit true biblical Christianity in these last days, it was a very difficult and bitter pill to swallow.

Many people ask me if I feel regret or bitterness. In all honesty, I can't find it in me to resent the past, but I feel a burden of responsibility towards all captives in the cults. We left many lovely God-fearing, but misguided, persons back at the Kingdom Hall who, because of Watchtower teaching, will no longer associate or even talk to us. But we still love them and want to help them. That, however, is the end of the story. Let's go back to the beginning.

Not for Me

In the early 1970s my mother and two sisters became Jehovah's Witnesses. Before long other relatives of mine became involved and were baptized as Witnesses. It was as if a religious wave had swept over my family. But my father, my two brothers and myself would have nothing to do with the Watchtower Society. In fact, we hated the effect they had on the family, especially when Christmas, birthdays, and Easter came around, though admittedly my motives were extremely selfish.

When I left school I joined the merchant navy and managed to escape the Jehovah's Witnesses' fervour—but only for a while. I eventually gave up the navy for a job ashore and started playing lead guitar in a rock and roll band, which kept me away from home for most evenings. Being away from my family so much was probably one factor that led my wife, Pam, to decide to take our little daughter and start attending the Kingdom Hall meetings with my mother and sisters. At the time she obviously enjoyed it, and one night when I happened to be in for a change, my wife tried to persuade me to go with her to the Kingdom Hall. Reluctant at first, I eventually consented and went. This was the start of my life in the organization. Before long I was studying and amassing volumes of Watchtower publications until I possessed a pretty impressive library of which I was proud.

Now Not for Her

Funnily enough, my wife eventually stopped going to the Kingdom Hall, and became quite opposed to my obsession with the organization. By contrast, I gave up the rock and roll band so that I could spend more time being 'theocratically' involved, which incurred the wrath of the other band members because I ruined a summer season by quitting. However, I thought I was putting God first and was baptized at a large district convention at Plymouth Argyle football ground.

As I became more knowledgeable I enjoyed the challenge of the preaching work and I just loved to use the Bible, the New World Translation of Jehovah's Witnesses of course, which, I was told at the time, was the most accurate of all Bibles. This didn't stop me collecting other Bible translations though and I found that they would often agree with each other but not with the New World Translation. However, rather than question the Watchtower Bible, I mistakenly came to the conclusion that Christendom's versions were corrupted by the clergy. After four years as a rank and file kingdom publisher going from door to door, I was appointed to the position of ministerial servant and given oversight of the literature account and the Kingdom Hall literature stock. I then got involved with teaching assignments, both at the Kingdom Hall and the home book study groups, all of which demanded so much time, but I liked it none the less.

Questions Raised

On a number of occasions I would call on people who raised serious questions about the Watchtower Society and their leaders. I recall one particular incident. I knocked at a door and the man who answered accused Charles Taze Russell, the Watchtower founder, of fraud, because he had sold phony 'miracle wheat'. Of course, I denied it and said he was mistaken. John, an elder of the Watchtower Society and a Jehovah's Witness for some forty years was waiting for me in his car. When I returned he asked me how the call went. I told him that the man was a lunatic, and what he had accused Russell of. John looked at me and said, 'It's true, Russell did sell phony wheat.' I was speechless, but John reassured me that it was a 'mistake' and that the Watchtower Society were still God's organization.

If this was an isolated instance it might have been forgotten, but over the years that followed, other house-holders would raise objections about the Society's teachings and false prophecies. The only defence was to claim that the people who said such things were 'evil slaves' and 'apostates' and that they deliberately told lies about God's organization. Jehovah's Witnesses are constantly reminded to ignore the remarks of these apostates and never ever read their literature. This worked with me for a few years but eventually, just by reading the Bible, which certainly could not be termed 'apostate', I could see that all was not well in Zion and many things disturbed me about Watchtower doctrine.

There were two main bones of contention that caused me to consider matters very carefully. The first was the fixing of a date for the Battle of Armageddon and the second was the method in which the 'great crowd' of Revelation chapter 7 were to be made perfect without being born again of God's Spirit. I thought our sinful flesh was corrupt and that no amount of striving would ever make it perfect (Jn 6:63). But as a loyal Jehovah's Witness I would always listen to the Society and shelve my doubts until the answer came through the Governing Body, the only channel from God. In the meantime I would simply plod on.

Over the years I called on many persons who raised alternative explanations for Scripture. I have had many in-depth studies and discussions with Christadelphians, Seventh Day Adventists, Mormons, and others, but I found that after a while I could defeat these objectors on a number of points. I tended always to attack the weakest point in my opponent's argument. I remember Christadelphians fell short when they denied Satan's personality and the pre-human existence of Jesus. The Adventists fell short because of Jewish law-keeping and Mormons fell short on just about everything. Defeating these opponents did my ego good and only served to make me think that the Jehovah's Witnesses had the truth, well 80 per cent of the time anyway.

Those Born Again Christians

However, one group that really challenged me were the 'born again' Christians with their 'know-so' salvation. Through articles in *The Watchtower* I was taught to have a strong aversion to the doctrines of the Trinity and hell, among others, and this gave me fuel for the fire. In my home town of Truro, born again Christians often took to the streets with tracts, booklets and large slogans commending Jesus and I made it my business to go gunning for them with my Bible. Some of them were inexperienced, and detecting this I'd browbeat them with talk of creeds, fourth-century controversies, and Jesus saying that 'the Father is greater than I'. But the church elders and pastors knew their stuff and I would often go home to study up. on different points, and sometimes they too would have to look up points to counter my arguments.

This carried on for about three years. In that time I got to know many born again Christians and a few became good friends. But I would always stand my ground and refuse to accept 'apostate' literature. While I had trust in the Watchtower Society, I would always meet any criticism and objections with Watchtower counter-arguments. Liberation from the organization would not come until my confidence in it was undermined and the truth about the Watchtower Society revealed.

As time went by other things about the Watchtower Society began to disturb me. Because I was the literature servant in our congregation, I was always given platform assignments to promote the literature campaigns and to encourage my fellow Witnesses to buy the Society's literature 'offer for the month' so they could sell it on the doors. I remember that on several occasions the Watchtower Society promoted the sale of older, out-dated publications to the public. Information on 1975 for sale in the late 1980s is money for old rope and financial gain could be the Society's only aim and not promoting the truth.

Another point that caused me a great problem was the rapidity with which the Society changed or modified their doctrines. When the Watchtower Society released their new two-volume Bible Commentary, *Insight on the Scriptures*, I found, even before it was released at the district assembly, that several teachings contained in it were already out-dated by articles in *The Watchtower* magazine. It is ironic that this new commentary was out of date even before it was available to Jehovah's Witnesses. This caused me to conclude that the 'increased light' syndrome of the Society was out of control. By 1989 my conscience was really disturbed, but what could I do but grin and bear it and pretend that all was well?

Awake! To The Watchtower

All this was to change when, one day in early 1989, I was walking in Truro town centre and a book entitled *Awake! To the Watchtower* caught my eye. I went into the shop and browsed through the book, but put it back on the shelf because this surely was apostate literature. However, I couldn't get it out of my mind and so I returned a couple of days later and against my conscience bought it. Reading the book in secret, because I knew I should not be taking in this information, I discovered that the Jehovah's Witness book *Reasoning from the Scriptures* that we used to 'prove' our doctrines was useless because it was full of pseudo-scholarship and misquotes. I then noticed that in the back of *Awake! To the Watchtower*, another book was advertised entitled *Crisis of Conscience* by Ray Franz. I'd heard of this book a couple of years previously, on a radio chat show, when Ray Franz was interviewed, and knew it was the story of an ex-member of the Governing Body of Jehovah's Witnesses. As I'd come this far I thought 'what the heck' and wrote to Reachout Trust for a copy.

In my letter I did not let on that I was a Jehovah's Witness, and when the book arrived, I gasped at the large gold sticker on the front of the parcel with 'Release to the Captives' and 'Christian Ministry to the Cults' written on it. I was afraid. Suppose another Witness was at my place when the parcel came and he saw it? He might tell the elders. Such is the power that the Watchtower Society have over the mind, especially the fear instilled by the thought of disfellowshipping. Anyway, I was not detected by my Witness relatives and friends who visited me frequently. I started to read both *Awake! To the Watchtower* and *Crisis of Conscience*. I just couldn't stop reading even though I found the information hard to take in. I was devastated, sick, upset, frightened, yet forced to admit error, and I came to realize that I could not trust the

Watchtower Society or view them in the same way ever again.

At this time, because of financial burdens, I had to take up two jobs. One job was from 9 pm to 6 am, after which I would rush home, change and go to my next job from 7 am to 10 am. This dual employment lasted for six weeks and physically drained me. Not only was I working long hours; I could not get much sleep anyway due to the turmoil in my mind and the conflicts bottled up inside. I was at my lowest point ever.

Secretly Desperate

Out of desperation, but still in secret, I wrote to Reachout Trust and explained my situation. I received back some letters that began to help pick me up. I would pray alone and admit to God, 'I'm confused. Help me. What am I to do? Please Jehovah, help me.' Emotion would grab me and I would be almost in tears, which is totally against my normal way of handling problems.

Then, one day, I visited my mother who, by this time, had been a staunch Jehovah's Witness for fourteen years. She'd just returned from the preaching work and rattled on about the lovely calls they'd had that morning. I couldn't stand it any more. I made her promise to keep quiet if I told her something, and she agreed. Then I just choked up that it would be only a matter of time before I would be leaving the organization. She was dumb-struck and extremely upset, but she didn't let on to the elders even though she thought that I was going mentally ill. Eventually I told my brother-in-law the same and he was flabbergasted and incredulous, but again he never talked to anyone, except my mother who already knew.

Meetings at the Kingdom Hall were unbearable and flat, devoid of spiritual refreshment. I made excuses to get out of speaking on the platform and going door to door. I even failed to put in the required 'hours' report for the last two months before I left the organization.

I couldn't stand the silence any more and took steps to bring my torment to a close. My mother and Bob, my brother-in-law, visited me at home and I explained my situation, substantiating my reasons for being disillusioned with the Watchtower Society from the Bible, photocopies of Watchtower false prophecies, and so on. I showed Bob that the Witnesses' claim that Jesus returned in 1914 is a lot of old nonsense and that Christ received His kingdom in the first century. He was convinced of the truth of this and made notes to take home for restudy.

At the end of the next meeting I approached Andrew, an elder who I knew had certain reservations on some of the Society's teachings. In times past Andrew and I would openly discuss uncertain teaching, such as the significance of 1914. I asked him to come round to my place as I needed to speak with him urgently. When he came, I told him of my plans to leave the organization. He, too, was really taken aback and offered to give help with my problems. He promised not to tell the other elders, but was to come round during the week to start a secret rehabilitation programme. Before he left that evening he called for restraint on my part, and I reluctantly agreed.

Blow Up

At this point things suddenly started to blow up because Bob, with the new-found information I'd passed to him, couldn't keep quiet about it like I had. Bob openly challenged other congregation members, using points from his own purchased copy of *Awake! To the Watchtower*. The elders soon got wind of what was happening, gathered together a posse and stormed around to his place. Bob was able to defeat them scripturally and defend his position. Finally, they demanded his keys to the Kingdom

Hall (Bob was the hall servant) and asked for his resignation as ministerial servant. Bob told them, 'You don't have to worry, you'll have my resignation from the organization in the morning.' Then they left.

The next day I was in line for a surprise visit by two different elders. Peter and Paul called on me and started asking me probing questions about my views of the Society. Peter was an arrogant, haughty man, and in response to his questions I purposely drew him out by saying, 'I think I've been brainwashed by the Society.' Boy, this was what he wanted, so I gave it to him. He was looking for something to nail me for, so I just thought 'try this for size'. It worked, and they left my house to tell the other elders.

Meanwhile, Andrew visited me again. By now I was convinced of the deity of Christ and told him so. He was agitated and couldn't answer my arguments taken from the material from Reachout. He departed, never to return, and threw in his lot with the Society, even though he disagreed with them on a number of points.

Suddenly, I was asked to appear before a judicial hearing of three elders, to which I agreed. I wasted no more time and let them have it, lock, stock and barrel, denouncing everything from Watchtower lies to false prophets. Then, to my shock, an elder, John, asked me, 'Do you still want to be a JW and carry on in your ministerial position? It's there if you want it.' I couldn't believe my ears. Poor Bob had virtually been thrown to the lions a few days previously. Now, here I was, openly calling the Society liars and false prophets, and they are telling me I can still be a Jehovah's Witness if I want. John said, 'You haven't been going around upsetting the congregation with what you know, so you haven't promoted a sect or anything.' What double standards! I replied firmly, 'I want no part with the Watchtower Society ever again.' After that I left, and just as I went out of the Kingdom

Hall door they shook my hand and said, 'Goodbye, and if we can ever be of help, don't hesitate to call.' Hypocrites, I thought! The next time they see me they'll walk by and ignore me. And, of course, they all ignore me to this day.

Leaving the chronological events for a minute and looking back from where I am now, I believe that the three elders on the committee deliberately tried to make a deal with me. If I had been willing to ignore the things that I had found out and just gone on as before, they would have been prepared to do the same. But how could I commit intellectual suicide in this way—to play false, to be transformed from one who had been deceived to one who knowingly deceives? No! No! No! I could not do it. My mind balked at the very idea. We were supposed to be 'in the truth'.

Sometimes I shudder to think of how many other Witnesses facing this same situation have recanted under pressure and closed their minds. Today there must be elders, ministerial servants, and many others, teaching things that they know to be false. I believe such persons are in a small minority within the Watchtower Society, but the thought that even one or two once basically honest Jehovah's Witnesses have been persuaded to become deceivers through organizational pressure is tremendously stressful.

I believe that the three elders cross-examining me on the judicial committee acted the way they did because of a mentality produced by years spent on the constant treadmill of Watchtower life. Anything is expendable for the sake of the organization—yes, even truth is expendable. I remember clearly how, after putting some of my findings regarding false prophecy to the committee, they evaded the issue rather than face it. John, one of the elders, resorted to the standard retreat excuse, saying, 'Yes, but what were we doing during the wars? Witnesses are neutral.'!

Over the years I've heard many Witnesses resort to this argument when quizzed on the doorstep, but I couldn't consent to this constant hiding behind baseless retreat arguments. For instance, I know that Christadelphians are a cult and hold to many false teachings, but does the fact that they (like Jehovah's Witnesses) refuse to go to war justify matters? What difference does it make if one is a pacifist false prophet? He is still a false prophet none the less.

I have since learned that this process of running from an issue that could undermine the organization is called 'think stop' by cult exit counsellors and is common in all the cults. But grace has delivered me from such powerful darkness. Today, as a born again son of God, I can face all issues head on in the light, confident that I am walking with a loving Saviour, who conquered my darkness (1 Jn 1:7).

Mum and Bob

Returning to the narrative, the next matter for the elders was to deal with my mother, but they didn't get a look in when they phoned her to make an appointment. She told them, 'I'm out, I want no part with that regime.' So now, Bob, Mum and I are out of the organization, but where else are we to go? I thought I would pay my 'born again' friends a visit at their church, and that's what I did. I was made most welcome, but was puzzled at the format of the service—it was unlike anything I had ever seen. Tom, one of the church elders whom I knew from past encounters in the street, was a great help to me and came to my house often, to chat about the Word, the Spirit and Christ.

I asked Christ into my heart and accepted Him as my personal Lord and Saviour. I came to realize that I had been born again of the Spirit. Hallelujah! Before long, Mum and Bob also came to the Christian Fellowship, accepted Christ and were born again in the Spirit—a double Hallelujah! Then a person named Peter who had been studying with the Jehovah's Witnesses for over three years but who, for some reason, had never been baptized, came and sought me out to find out why I had left the organization. I told him; he went down the shop, purchased a copy of *Awake! To the Watchtower*, forsook the organization and now comes to church with us.

Reaching Out

Today, we four rejoice in the Lord and are burdened for those in the cults. Our whole Christian Fellowship feels a definite calling in the Spirit to the cults and we are having a major impact here in the Truro area. I am confident that Mum, Bob, Peter and myself are just the first-fruits to Christ from the cults in our area. In fact, we are already helping some who are studying with the Jehovah's Witnesses. It's exciting work: it glorifies God, it liberates captives and we just want to reach out to others for Christ.

As I conclude my testimony thus far, I look back and feel I've come a long way. I've been hurt deep in my heart but by God's grace I've been raised from the Watchtower grave of deception to a new life in Christ. I just want to praise God for His mercy, grace and love. And I mustn't forget to thank Doug Harris from Reachout Trust for his devotion and ministry to those captive in the cults.

In the days and years ahead I will use my life and resources to reach out to those in bondage. I rejoice in my deliverance, and that joy is increased more and more as I see other Jehovah's Witnesses set free to serve Christ.

Trying To Be A Worthy Mormon

Brian Rendell

I was a Mormon, or, to be more accurate, a member of the Latter-day Saints, for eight years. Indeed, I was not just a 'run of the mill' Mormon—I became one of the top members in the south-west of England area. My credentials included an invitation to speak in Salt Lake City, the world headquarters, and a Temple Recommend (more about that later), but all this counted for nothing when the Lord decided it was time for me to join His family.

Mormons, on the whole, are very nice people: they have impeccable manners, a moral code second to none, a welfare system that works, and some truth in the message they bring to you. However, please heed the warning not to believe everything they say because there are serious flaws in their doctrine, as is the case for all sects and cults. The more truth employed by the Mormon the easier it is for the listener to accept it and be swayed into thinking that any inaccuracies could just be a lack of knowledge on the part of the investigator (the Mormon name for the person they are trying to indoctrinate).

Getting Involved

I first became involved with the Mormons in 1980. I lived on an estate that had a very bad reputation, and my wife and I had been discussing the best way to bring up our two

25

daughters, then aged eight and one. We had come to the conclusion that using our own knowledge and in our own strength there wasn't any way we could succeed, and so, as you can imagine, we were becoming desperate.

One day, as I arrived home from work, I was greeted with the news that my wife had been talking with the Mormons and they would be coming back the next day to see us both. However, it was only a couple of hours later when they appeared at our door again. They said that the story my wife had told them had so moved them that they had returned to their lodgings and prayed about our situation. These are their exact words, 'The Lord has laid it upon our hearts that we should return immediately and give you this tract.' The title of the tract was 'Why stay morally clean?' This seemed like the answer to our quest. Naturally, we let the Mormons into our home, and with our desperate need for something to hold on to we soon became trapped in their web. Everything they said had enough of the truth to make it acceptable to us, because we had nothing to use as a comparison. I had been to church until I was fifteen but had found it boring and had retained very little biblical knowledge.

Later, as a Mormon, I too would use this type of approach, which works with many people. Being in pairs, as one talks the other one observes. If you distract the talker, the other one, called his companion, will instantly take up where the first faltered. This ploy is something Mormons are well trained for: the first member of the team throws many situations and ideas at you, the second notes anything that causes even a slight reaction. They exploit it to gain entry, and also your confidence, which is an excellent sales technique.

Priest and Elder

For now, however, I was the one learning, and I was doing very well. Not long after I was baptized as a Mormon, I was made a priest, which entitled me to perform communion, or sacrament as they call it. I very quickly absorbed all that was required of me, including tithing, and within a few months I was made an elder of the church. Now I could anoint others with oil, give blessings and conduct a complete service. I was revered by those around me and there was no position in the Mormon Church that I could not hold; the only qualification was to be 'worthy'. This word was to haunt me throughout my time with the Mormons.

I found that to be 'worthy' meant initially that I had to pay 10 per cent of my gross income to the church. Then, on the first Sunday of every month, all adults fasted (except the sick or aged) and the money saved on food was paid into another account. There was also a missionary account, and once again to be 'worthy' meant you had to contribute to that. Another requirement was that all members gave towards the upkeep of church premises etc, and yet another was to help towards the provision of learning books and tracts used in the door-to-door work. When you worked it all out, something in the order of 20 per cent of your gross income went directly to the church—and that was the minimum. All that just to be 'worthy'.

In the Temple

Now let me say a little more about the coveted 'Temple Recommend' because it is every good Mormon's ambition to have one. This allows you to go into any of the thirty or so Mormon temples in the world. Although there are many Mormon buildings, there is only one temple in Britain. Once I had been an elder for a minimum of a year, I was in a position to be considered for this prized piece of paper, but it was something that I had to work hard to obtain. In the south-west there were 3,000 registered Mormons but only about 200 had this prized recommend.

To obtain the recommend you first have to be considered 'worthy' by your local leaders, and even before the process is put into action, you have a series of six or eight lessons to let you know what will be expected of you and what you might expect. Then you have an interview with your local leader. This interview is very formal and can take up to three hours—mine certainly did. It is undertaken in complete secrecy and no records are kept. There are fifteen questions that you have to answer, mostly about your willingness to obey leaders locally, nationally and internationally. You are also questioned about 'worthiness' in regard to tithing. However, the leader already knows the position because complete and up to date records are kept of every penny that every Mormon donates. I know this for a fact because I kept these records for four years.

If all goes well in this first interview you are handed a docket with one signature on it. You then have to move on to be interviewed by the Stake President (this position is like that of a regional manager) and here the whole process is repeated. Once you have succeeded in persuading this second man that you are ready, you have a second signature added to your piece of paper and it's *off to the temple*! The British one is at Lingfield, Surrey. All that happens inside the temple is called 'sacred' and must never be revealed to any other person; it cannot even be discussed by those who have had the experience and have the recommends. After my first visit to the temple I was so excited that I started talking about it on the way home. The driver stopped on the motorway and told me to get out because I was breaking the Mormon taboo.

When you first visit the temple you have to go to the clothing store, which is not part of the temple, and there you must purchase underwear, referred to as 'garments'. These have odd markings on both breasts, the tummy and the right thigh—very similar symbolism to that of the Freemasons. You must also buy or hire white robes, a green apron, a white sash and a white beret for men or a white bonnet and veil for the women. You also need a pair of white shoes with white soles, none of which you can purchase without your Temple Recommend.

At the temple doors you have to show your Temple Recommend—without it you are not admitted. I remember that one time I went through the door without the person on the door being able to see my Temple Recommend. Immediately, I had to step outside again, never leaving the sight of the person on the door, and produce my Temple Recommend. The Temple Recommend is dated and stamped because it has to be renewed annually (perhaps you become unworthy!).

You book in and first-timers are given a ticket to pin to their clothing to identify them as newcomers who don't know the routine. The first time you go through the temple you do it for your own endowment. At this time you have only a sheet, called a shield, to cover your nakedness. You are ceremoniously washed, and in a forty-five-second period you are given thirty promises, supposedly from the Lord. Now you are worthy to put on your garments. These consist of a T-shirt with a V-neck and pants that reach the knees, with the strange marks mentioned above.

Dressed, you proceed to the endowment room for what, in my day, was a two-hour session. There you receive various secret handshakes, make certain vows and perform various signs. The gist of all this is a warning that you must not reveal anything that goes on in the Temple. Just before you go into the endowment room you are

given a new name which you must not reveal to anyone;
mine was Mormon.

Baptism for the Dead

On subsequent visits, when you go through the process,
you go through it for someone who is dead. One at a time
you approach the veil, where the answer to the first question, 'What is the first token of the Aaronic priesthood?',
is your own Christian name or that of the dead person you
are representing. This ceremony of baptism for the dead
goes on for fourteen hours a day, five-to-six days a week,
in every Temple in the world. Where do all the names of
these dead people come from? They are supplied by members tracing their family trees and having them recorded in
Utah. Not only do the Mormons undertake the act of
baptism for the dead but they proceed to accept them
completely into the Mormon faith, because they believe
that their church is the only true church and alone has
absolute authority to do just as they please. Once again, I
beg you to please beware of these people because they
have no respect for anyone not with them; they believe
they have unlimited power to do as they think without
consultation.

On many occasions during my time with the Mormons I
did things which were certainly not Christian. For
instance, one time while I was keeping the financial
records I discovered that we were short of the amount
required to purchase the books and tracts needed for the
following year. With a fellow Mormon I hatched a plan to
raise some cash quickly! On the following Sunday I
announced that the Lord had revealed to me that all
present at that meeting should pay an extra and special
tithe so that the work for the following year could go
forward promptly. At the end of the meeting every person
was interviewed and told the amount the Lord wanted

him or her to give; everyone paid in full before leaving that meeting. Another example of misusing my position was when I was teaching a group of ladies to prepare them to be ready to go to the Temple. I counselled one newly married young woman that she should abstain from sexual relations with her husband for three months to prove to the Lord that she was 'worthy'. She did!

As you can see, both cases were man-inspired, and I have had many sleepless nights remembering the times I tried to do God's work without even consulting Him. I now know that I have been forgiven by God, and I have learned to forgive myself, which was the hardest part because I am human. God loves us with His agape love that most of us find very hard to understand.

Doubts About the 'True Church'

Being involved in the continuous routine of Mormonism keeps your mind occupied, but from time to time there is still the possibility of doubts creeping in. My first doubts about whether the Mormons were really the true church or not came on a day when we received a decree from Utah telling us that in future the *Book of Mormon* was to be the first book of the Mormons and the Bible would only be a companion to it.

This was soon followed by the death of the then 'prophet' of the church, Spencer W. Kimball. Without a prophet the church had no head. The three men of the First Presidency took over until the Twelve Apostles could elect a new prophet; it had to be a unanimous decision I was told. I really felt that one of the younger men would take over to give fresh leadership to the church, but I was assured that Ezra B. Taft would be the new prophet. No divine revelation was to be involved; he was to be appointed simply because he was the senior member. This caused doubt number two.

Doubt number three was personal. I began to question the Mormon Church in general: what they believed, how they lived their lives, and so on. In fact, I began to question so much and the pressure became so intense that I suffered a nervous breakdown.

So May 1986 saw me attending a psychiatric day hospital. I joined a very intense group which attempted to break down your inhibitions and mental barriers. After one very hectic session two ladies invited me to go to a particular church with them. What was so amazing about this was that neither of them belonged to that fellowship and neither knew that the other had asked me, yet they asked within minutes of each other. Nor did they know that for the previous six weeks or so, every Sunday evening I had stood outside one of our local churches, one with born again Christians who were active against the Mormons, but I never had the courage to go in. I had been at the doors so many times, but now I had received two invitations within minutes to go inside that very church.

Salvation

I accepted their invitation and on the following Sunday, 2nd November, we met outside Holy Trinity Church, even though I had been at the Mormon meeting from 8 am until 12 noon that day. It was like nothing I had experienced before—people walking about greeting one another with genuine feelings, people enjoying the praise, and so on. During the evening someone spoke in tongues, which seemed very odd to me, then a translation was given, the basis being 2 Corinthians 6:18. Immediately I began to shake uncontrollably and Tricia, my friend, observed that the message was for me and that the Holy Spirit was trying to attract my attention. I was terrified and all I could think was, 'I'm a Mormon.' Tricia said that

I should go forward because the message was meant for me. In the end she lead me by the hand to the front and told Adrian, the vicar, who I was and how the Holy Spirit was affecting me. Adrian prayed over me and more than one person said they witnessed a black cat leave me and go out of the church.

At the end of the service I was invited into the vestry with a number of the church members and my friend. They all prayed in tongues and to my utter amazement I found myself on the floor. Adrian then told me that to become a Christian I would have to publicly denounce Mormonism, and I would have to do so before Christmas, just eight weeks away.

At the time I was attending the day hospital five full days a week; I met the psychiatrist for two hours every week; I had a history of abusing prescribed drugs; and I was taking more than twenty different types of pills—to help me to sleep, to wake up, to relax, etc. You name it, I was trying it. You can see that I was in a real mess.

However, the very night that I had been to the church I went home and wrote a letter to the Mormons enclosing my highly valued Temple Recommend and telling them that I no longer wished to be associated with them. A couple of days later, with the help of a friend, I returned ten cardboard boxes of documents, including membership records, to the local Mormon church! Two weeks later I stood before my new Christian fellowship and denounced Mormonism and all that it represented. Even so, for six months enormous pressure was put on me to return to the Mormons. They even sent the children I had taught in Sunday School to ask me when I was coming back.

Fully Delivered

From that day I have only returned to the psychiatric day hospital to say goodbye and tell them that I would not be coming any more, and more recently to deliver a Christmas card. I have not taken even one psychiatric drug, sleeping pill or any other form of medication from that time. I cancelled my weekly visit to the psychiatrist and have never been back. The Lord released me from all my bondage, including Mormonism, in one very exciting evening. It hasn't always been easy but I make it through by knowing that the Holy Spirit lives in me and that my best friend is Jesus Christ, my Saviour, who died on the cross that I might be saved.

Since my conversion I have been reminded a number of times by local Mormons of the vows I took to keep quiet about the secret Temple ceremonies and that I should beware of the consequences of my actions. What they don't realize is that now I am a son of God and what He wants I will give. At the moment He requires me to let it be known that the Mormons are definitely not the true church of Jesus Christ.

Recently, one of the leaders of the Mormon Church had the cheek to warn me that he would be my judge on Judgement Day. He also reminded me that because of his exalted position on earth he will go to the celestial kingdom, and that he and his wife will become gods, just as Jesus is a God, and they will have their own world to rule. The whole idea is that the harder a Mormon works and the more he achieves, the higher his status after death.

There is more I could say, but I leave it here with the promise that any questions that are unanswered I will answer if you contact me through Reachout Trust. I believe that God gave me my experience with the Mormons so that I could help those who feel trapped and can see no way out. Do not despair. We can help you to help yourselves, because God loves you and wants you to know the full truth.

Obedient To Jehovah's Organization

Jean Norris

In 1986 I divorced my husband; I won't go into all the details about that time except to say that Ray was making my life and the lives of our four sons so miserable that I felt I could not go on living with him. However, I still loved him and on several occasions we tried for a reconciliation, but each time, after just a few days, it would become obvious that he had not changed and we would go our separate ways again. All this was tearing us apart, until I felt that life was not worth living.

Belief in God

I had always believed in God, and I always prayed to Him, having been brought up by a mother who was a Roman Catholic and a father who belonged to the Church of England. One morning, during an attempt at one of our hopeless reconciliations, I stood at the kitchen window looking out over the hills, and I cried out to God, 'What is the point of living? Why is there nothing but misery?'

With no apparent answers forthcoming, I got into the routine of the day and walked the boys to school. All the other mums were chatting as I watched the boys go into school, but I didn't want to talk to anyone—I just wanted to be left alone. I did, however, notice a little old lady who was also alone and somehow she ended up walking

35

along the road with me. She talked about how different the world was now compared with the time when she had sent her children miles to school all alone; now it was not safe to let them out at all. I had to agree, and as we went along she started to tell me that the Bible warns us that the world will become worse in the last days. With dismay I realized that she was a Jehovah's Witness. I knew without doubt who she was because my mother had warned me about Jehovah's Witnesses all my life.

While I was racking my brains to think of a polite way to escape from this little old lady without being rude, I suddenly remembered the words I had spoken to God Himself only fifteen minutes before. With a real shock I believed with all my heart that He was giving me the answer, and I had better listen. I bit hook, line and sinker.

Bible Study

I didn't have just a one-hour 'Bible study' per week as many do; I studied with Flo, the sweet old lady, every weekday morning. In fact, I couldn't get enough study to satisfy me. I went through the Watchtower books so fast that I couldn't afford to buy them, so Flo would buy them and give them to me as gifts, and I even got some really old ones from Flo that I shouldn't have had.

Flo had been 'in the truth' for over twenty years and had zealously pioneered for some time. I tried to emanate her zealousness and went to all the meetings each week— five hours in total. If I had to miss just one I felt very guilty. But someone would always come to see why I had missed and I thought that was because they loved me. I rejoiced the day that the elders felt I had proved myself worthy and I was at last allowed to go out on the door-to-door work.

Not only was I zealous, but I knowingly used the same techniques that Flo used on me to indoctrinate my three youngest sons. However, my eldest would have none of it, and became quite rebellious. I witnessed without mercy to everyone I met, until my lovely mum ended up not speaking to me for a period of about four weeks around Christmas, which we didn't celebrate, along with birthdays or any other holiday.

Hatred of Sin

When through the Bible I found that sin was disobedience to Jehovah, I immediately stopped doing any known sin that I might be committing. And of course I became totally obedient to Jehovah's organization. I loved God so much, and I wanted to please Him more than anything, and if that meant being obedient to His organization and being separate from everybody else, then that was what I had to do regardless of the hurt. I hated sin and I became very self-righteous.

Right at the beginning I told Ray that if he would become part of the organization, we could remarry and be a family again. What I hadn't known at the time was that Ray had become a born again Christian and been filled with the Holy Spirit at the age of fifteen. He had actually grown as a Christian for about two years but because of opposition from his friends and family he backslid. So here was I offering what he wanted most in the world, and a way out of his mountainous debt problem, and all he had to do was deny Jesus and join the Watchtower. But even though Ray had sunk so low in every other way, he could not do that. The elders therefore advised me that if Ray would not come into 'the truth', I should let him go completely.

No Defence

Unfortunately, another reason that Ray had backslid in the first place was that he never read his Bible, and he could not defend his faith. Realizing this, he went back to his old Pentecostal church to get help for me and the children, and he recommitted his life to Jesus. He also now agreed that we should not be living together as man and wife as we were divorced, so he moved back into his flat. We were separated again and I became more and more involved in the organization, but found myself being constantly woken up at night by a terrifying presence. I told Flo about this and she got two of the elders to come and 'pray' about it. It didn't stop after that—in fact it got worse. The only conclusion the elders could come to was that Ray was bringing demons with him when he visited the children on Sunday afternoons.

Around this time I became so tired through lack of sleep, going to all the meetings, and feeling constantly guilty, that I told Ray that if he mentioned the name of Jesus again in my house, I would throw him out and never let him back in. It wasn't long before he did mention Jesus again and, looking back, I guess I really provoked him into it. True to my word though I ordered him out, never to return.

After three weeks it looked as if he wasn't coming back, and in my heart I missed him, but Armageddon could come at any time and I had to remain loyal to Jehovah and His organization. Before long, though, he was once again visiting us every Sunday after church and I was certainly glad. He didn't have an easy time of it because I would batter him with Scripture, twisted scriptures of the Watchtower Society of course, and we would end up arguing. But I was the one doing all the shouting. Since Ray had returned to the Lord and remained faithful to Him, I could see that he was a different man, more like the one I had married in the first place, However, I thought that if he would not turn to Jehovah then we could never be together. Yet there was clearly something about Ray that was really different. I could only describe it as peace. He still couldn't argue the Scriptures with me, but from time to time the Holy Spirit would give him perhaps just one sentence that would pierce my heart. Although I never let any reaction show on my face at the time, I would be searching the Scriptures as soon as he had gone.

I Must Be Right

One time in particular I remember so clearly. We were discussing a point and I said, 'We both believe we are right, but one of us has to be wrong. Are you humble enough to admit that it might be you?' Sitting there with my smug attitude a voice added in my ear, 'And are you humble enough to admit if it is you?' The voice was so gentle and yet my heart melted. But I knew I was the one that was right! Didn't I?

After three weeks Ray faithfully came again, not even knowing if I would open the door to him. But the Lord had been softening my heart and opening my eyes to things in the organization that I tried to ignore but just couldn't. I saw things in the Bible that I couldn't understand and no one could or would give me a satisfactory answer about them. Why would Jesus tell such a misleading parable as that recorded in Luke 16:19–31? If He knew very well that there was no such place as a fiery hell, had He made a mistake? If the souls mentioned in Revelation 6:9–11 were dead, how could they be crying out? And how could Jehovah have been in the garden talking to Adam when no man has seen God? I was told to put these kind of thoughts out of my mind, as they were the devil's attempt to subvert me, and I did really try to obey the Society and not to think about these and other scriptural puzzles. You might wonder how a person with any intelligence could fall for this. All I can say is, if you could tell when you were being brainwashed then no one ever would be brainwashed, and yet people regularly are when seeking God with no knowledge of the Bible.

At this point I started to notice a lack of patience on the part of the people I was questioning. I further detected for the first time a lack of love displayed by the gossip and backbiting. This lack was also shown up by some who had a very unkind attitude towards people not in the organization, some of whom were, after all, kinder than me for a start.

Those Pentecostals

About this time an article on Pentecostals appeared in *The Watchtower*, and of course it completely condemned them. When Ray came round the Sunday after I wanted him to read and explain the article. He said he would do so if I would read something of his. This is strictly forbidden by the organization but I so badly wanted Ray to read the *Watchtower* article that I eventually agreed to read his literature. As Ray left the house, he turned and asked me to promise to read it, as he had promised to read *The Watchtower*. Now I was torn. I had to promise. When he had gone, to satisfy my conscience, I literally flicked through the book he had left me in about three seconds, but I had seen something, in bold type: The Alpha and the Omega. During the following days I could not get that phrase out of my mind, although I didn't know what it meant.

Alpha and Omega

The following Tuesday night's book study meeting was on the Book of Revelation, and as we read I saw clearly that the Alpha and the Omega was Jehovah God. He was also the 'Beginning and the End' and 'the First and the Last'. That was all right then. That very same week I had further confirmation at the Thursday night ministry school at the Kingdom Hall. We were reading Isaiah 44 and again I saw that Jehovah God was indeed 'the First and the Last'. So far so good, but when I went back to Revelation to check things out my troubles restarted. I found that in chapter 1, verses 17 and 18, 'the First and the Last' had been dead, so surely this must be Jesus? The more I read the passage, the more it seemed to me that Jesus and Jehovah were one together. This was a new revelation to me, one which I couldn't understand.

I asked Jehovah to help me out of my confusion and He led me through the Kingdom Interlinear Translation from scripture to scripture. As I compared the side of the page giving the Greek and literal English Translations with the other side containing the New World Translation, I just knew. I remembered all the times I had argued with people and said that Jesus was not God. Alone in my bedroom, I asked Him to forgive me, and as I gave my life to Him, I knew that He was with me.

New Start

I knew that it was His voice I had heard and that He had waited patiently, because I was His, just as He waits for all who belong to Him. And I know that He is always with me. I actually became ill and was in bed for a week, during which time the Lord deprogrammed me with the aid of books and tracts that Ray was pleased to bring me.

Soon Ray took me to his church, the Assemblies of God in Wigan, and I found a truly loving and caring family. These people prayed me in. Within six months of my leaving the Watchtower, my four sons were also saved, and Ray and I remarried in church. Jesus has healed both

Ray and myself physically as well as spiritually, and even Ray's huge financial debt has been cleared. The Lord has done so much in our lives that I could never write it all down, and His mercies *are* new every morning. The thief came to steal, and kill, and destroy; *He* came that we might have life, and have it abundantly.

From Joseph Smith To Jesus Christ

Ann Thomas

I was raised in a home with high moral standards even though as a family we never went to church. In my teens I came to realize that there must be more to life; there had to be a purpose and I wanted to know God. I found my answers, so I believed, in the Church of Jesus Christ of Latter-day Saints, otherwise known as the Mormon Church. I met and married Mike, my husband, in the church, and our four children were born into it. We were both faithful members of the church—myself for eighteen years and my husband for fourteen, and we both served in many important positions. Being such dedicated Mormons, you may be able to imagine the tremendous shock waves we caused in the Mormon community when, in August 1986, we turned our backs on the Latter-day Saints in a period of only two weeks. The reason for that turn-around is what I want to share.

I'll Never Leave

Over the years as a Latter-day Saint I had talked with many people of other faiths, including Christians, and had never even considered leaving the Mormon Church. When people spoke to me about becoming a born again Christian there were two main reasons why I would not listen. First, they would usually start in the most obvious place by attacking those beliefs that made me different, like accepting the *Book of Mormon*. This immediately caused me to go on the defensive. It is very difficult to win people over when you begin by telling them how wrong they are and offending them. In 1 Corinthians 2:2 Paul resolved to know nothing except Jesus Christ and Him crucified, and that is a good guideline.

The second reason I would not listen is very subtle. Cults teach that they have received new, greater truths, and I would not listen because I felt superior, and pitied Christians because they had only the original teachings of the Bible, whereas my leaders had received greater knowledge. I could not see that these additional teachings were changing the truths in the Bible and that the simplicity of the gospel is all that is needed.

Read the Bible Alone

When you've been going along on one path for so many years it is difficult to suddenly admit you are on the wrong one, but what happened to me was a gradual realization that my faith was not working. My husband and I started discussing things, talking to people, and searching the Bible, all with the honest aim of putting things right in our lives and becoming better Mormons. There was a difference now though because we were reading the Scriptures with honest, open eyes, and not just with Mormon blinkers on. We started to find things that differed from the teachings of the Latter-day Saints, especially when we came to the letter to the Romans. I read about salvation by grace and not through anything that I could do, which is the opposite to the Mormon teaching of making oneself worthy by doing many things. I couldn't understand how I had not seen this before, but now I was addressing basic gospel principles and not arguing with someone over weird and wonderful points of doctrine. I was stripping away all the extra teachings added by the Mormon Church and was looking at the heart of the matter. It was a joy to read the Scriptures and be able to take them at face value instead of having to use a Mormon commentary to interpret them for me. I came to realize that I had accepted a lot of things blindly. The Mormons work on the principle that if you believe the church is true, you will believe what they say; because the church teaches it, you don't question it!

Question Sincerely

When I began to question and sincerely seek the truth it was like the floodgates opening, and within a very short time my husband and I both came to realize that although we had believed in Jesus Christ and tried to follow Him, we did not have a living relationship with Him, and despite all our efforts we were not saved. Fortunately we had an old friend with whom we had had many a heated debate over the gospel. He was a Christian and had tried in vain to show us the truth. Yet now, in our discussions, my husband and I had come to realize that something vital was missing in our lives. When we could not identify it we tried a new approach and asked ourselves, 'Who do we know who has got it?' The answer was immediate—our Christian friend John. Very cautiously we contacted him, and he came to see us.

We would spend hours talking to him, often past midnight, but as he shared the Scriptures with us, especially from Romans, the answer to our needs became obvious. I was to take the step of becoming a Christian on the 25th August 1986. But coming out of a cult isn't always as easy as it sounds. If we were to leave the Mormon Church, where were we to go? We had been taught that all other churches were not of God. Here John was to help us again.

John encouraged us to come and see what his church was really like. My husband Mike went first on his own to check it out very carefully. He came back so excited that he talked about nothing else for the whole week! He was actually saved the following Saturday, and couldn't wait to take the whole family the next day. At the morning meeting the moving of the Spirit was so strong that I couldn't handle it. I had to leave before the end and went outside and sobbed as if my heart was breaking. When we went back in the evening I was surprised to find that I was no longer upset and could respond to the Spirit. God had done a great work in me, and I was saved the following day. Here is an excerpt from my journal entry that night:

> Michael left me alone and I put my head in my hands and poured it all out to God. I didn't know what to say and I asked Him to help me. I told Him I had tried for so long to do the right things and never succeeded and I needed Him to do them. I asked Him in and asked Him to keep the promises I had been reading in the Scriptures, even though I didn't understand how they worked. Suddenly my tears stopped and I became peaceful and calm. Everything seemed to stop and it literally took my breath away. I remember thinking, 'If I don't breathe in a minute I shall faint.'

I called Michael back in. We looked at each other and I just said, 'He's here.' We hugged and I started crying again.

Salvation By Grace Not Works

Apart from the beauty and simplicity of salvation by grace, which the Mormon Church does not teach, the two things that struck me the most were what I call 'no separation' and 'no condemnation'. When the people of Israel worshipped at the Tabernacle, and later at the Temple, the Most Holy Place, where God dwelt, was veiled by a curtain—only the high priest could enter into the presence of God, and only once a year. That changed with the death of Christ. In Mark 15:37–38 we read:

> And Jesus uttered a loud cry, and breathed His last. And the veil of the temple was torn in two from top to bottom.

There is a chorus we sing, called 'All of you', which says:

> Torn in two
> The veil was torn in two
> And now I'm walking through
> No separation.

The Living Bible version of Hebrews 10:19 expresses it perfectly:

> And so, dear brothers, now we may walk right into the very Holy of Holies where God is, because of the blood of Jesus.

All Mormons who have been to a Mormon Temple wear special underwear called Temple garments which they hold to be very sacred and never take off, except to wash. So complete was the change in me that, to the astonishment of John, the following morning I threw my Temple garments in the bin. The following day I visited some dear Mormon friends to witness to them. My journal entry said, 'Two days a Christian and I couldn't keep it to myself.'

Up to the time we were actually saved, we were still seeking to become better Mormons, and it was quite a shock when one evening the realization dawned that we could no longer be Mormons at all. So much of what we now knew to be true was contrary to Mormon doctrine. We contacted our leader, called the 'bishop', and he visited us. He made no attempt to discuss with us the Scriptures and our understanding of them, but insisted that if we would attend the Mormon church regularly, read the Mormon scriptures more, and pay our tithing, God would bless us with understanding. After our reading of Romans this was so obviously a doctrine of works. I faced him and asked if, knowing what I now knew to be true, I could sit in a Mormon meeting and not be a hypocrite. He had to say, 'No.' There was nothing more to say.

Ostracized and Excommunicated

When the news broke it sent great shock waves through the local Mormon community, and my attempts to circulate a loving letter of explanation to everyone caused such upset that I had to stop. We expected our friends to rush to dissuade us and were surprised and hurt to find that instead they avoided us. Our two sons were attending the Mormon cub pack and were refused lifts home, and people would cross the street if they saw us coming. Only a few made the attempt to communicate, and for some of them it was simply an attempt to shore up their faith by proving us wrong. We later found out that the reason we were ostracized was fear; we had been so strong in the church and we left so suddenly that members were afraid to talk to us in case it was 'catching'.

We felt that we could not be baptized as Christians while we were still baptized as Mormons, so we both asked to be excommunicated. This is a very formal process involving a church court, and because Michael belonged to the priesthood—Mormon priesthood is open only to men—and held quite a high position in the local church, he had to submit to a 'higher court'. My court consisted of the bishop and his two counsellors. When the solemn sentence of excommunication was passed they were very surprised and uncomfortable because I grinned and said, 'Thank you very much!' In both our courts we had the opportunity to witness our new faith to the church leadership, and shortly afterwards we both had the opportunity to publicly renounce all connection with Mormonism, which was very important.

Now Made One

As a Mormon I always felt unworthy to come before God, and I was taught that only those who had obeyed all the laws and ordinances of the gospel might one day be righteous enough to live in God's presence. In John 14:6 Jesus said, 'No one comes to the Father, but through Me.' The cults put themselves between man and God. They teach, in effect, that you become acceptable to God by doing what they teach and participating in their ordinances. Joseph Smith, who founded the Mormon Church, said about the *Book of Mormon* that a man could get closer to God through this book than through any other book. The Mormons also have Temples which only those judged to be 'worthy' can go to, and there they learn secret words and signs to get into heaven. Ephesians 3:12 says, 'In him and through faith in him we may approach God with freedom and confidence' (NIV). I came to realize how simple it is to enter into the presence of God, and how it can be a present reality rather than just a future hope.

But there is a lesson here for Christians too. Never let anything come between you and God, and don't put anything in the way of others: not forms of worship, or dress, or whether you should drink alcohol, or even minor points of doctrine. We are supposed to be one body, so let us concentrate on our similarities rather than our differences. In 1 Samuel 16:7 we are told that man looks on the outward appearance but God looks on the heart. A wise man once said, 'The heart of the matter is the matter of the heart.' It is not up to us to judge. Let us live together in Christian unity and have no separation either between ourselves or between us and God. Remember that Paul taught in Romans 8:38–39 that nothing will ever be able to separate us from the love of God.

Why Get Involved?

You may be wondering why I joined the Mormon Church in the first place. There are two main reasons. The first can be summed up in the phrase of my house group leader, Rob, used: 'The good is the greatest enemy of the best.' The Mormon Church has a lot of good in it, and teaches some truth and a lot of things that are close to the truth. Through this they deceive many people into thinking they have it all, and seekers do not recognize the errors. Most cults are the same.

The best way to show up a counterfeit is to put the real thing next to it. There is no argument like a vital, living relationship with Jesus Christ. We need to make sure that we have such a relationship. Then we need to make sure that it shows.

Checklist for God

The second reason the Mormon Church attracted me is that it is very appealing to be presented with a set of commands to follow in order to be acceptable to God. To feel that salvation will be guaranteed if I complete a checklist makes life very simple. Things such as relationships and attitudes seem much too difficult and uncertain, especially when you believe that you cannot know if you are saved until Judgement Day. It seemed much easier to keep a list of rules. Only later did the reality turn out not to be so simple. The problem is that we have such good intentions but because of human nature we do not live up to them. Every failure makes it a possibility that you will fall short when you are judged. Everyone watches everyone else, and you feel God is keeping a checklist of your actions. The burden of guilt and condemnation became so great at times that I stopped praying, because I couldn't face God at all, and eventually this was a major reason for my crisis of faith. I couldn't see how a loving God could have intended for me to live like that.

Hot, Warm, or Caffeine?

The Mormon teaching on salvation and grace is that when you face the judgement bar, God's grace will make up the difference. The trouble with this is that you don't know how much righteousness is enough. This also leads to controversy about the exact interpretation of rules. After all, if they are going to get you into heaven, you want to make sure you get them right. An example is the Mormon health law, called the Word of Wisdom. It included advice against having hot drinks. When the advice was not universally accepted it was made into a commandment. Then there was the problem of defining 'hot drinks'. Did it mean all drinks had to be only warm, or even cold, or did it refer to a particular hot drink? The members wondered why, since no reason was given. Then medical science discovered that tea and coffee contain caffeine, which can be harmful, so many members accepted that as God's reason for the ban. The trouble with that conclusion is that there is now a controversy over whether God wants them to ban Coca-Cola as well, because it contains more caffeine than tea and coffee!

Woe to you lawyers as well! For you weigh men

down with burdens hard to bear, while you
yourselves will not even touch the burdens with one
of your fingers (Lk 11:46).

No condemnation and no separation go hand in hand
here, because these things end up coming between you
and God instead of bringing you closer.

Part of the Mormon creed says:

We believe that through the atonement of Christ all
mankind may be saved by obedience to the laws and
ordinances of the gospel.

Imagine then how I felt when I read scriptures such as
Romans 3:20–22:

...by the works of the Law no flesh will be justified
in His sight; for through the Law comes the knowledge of sin. But now apart from the Law the righteousness of God has been manifested, being
witnessed by the Law and the Prophets.

When I discovered Romans 8:1, 'There is therefore
now no condemnation for those who are in Christ Jesus',
it affected me so deeply that I could not get it out of my
mind for days, and eventually wrote a song about it.

What a joy it is to read verses such as John 3:17–18:

For God did not send the Son into the world to judge
the world, but that the world should be saved
through Him. He who believes in Him is not judged.

And Philippians 3:9:

Not having a righteousness of my own derived from
the Law, but that which is through faith in Christ,

the righteousness which comes from God on the basis of faith.

I found that Christ can lift the burden of guilt and not only make me clean and acceptable, but give me the power to obey.

No Condemnation

Christians need to be reminded of these verses too. We can so easily fall into the trap of feeling condemned when we fail. We must remember that we do not need to try harder, but to learn to submit and give God free rein in our lives. I no longer feel as though God is watching me with a checklist. Now He is on my side and we sort out my weaknesses together. To go back to the chorus 'All of you', it says:

> No condemnation
> I hold my head up high
> You gave your life that I
> Might live in you
> In celebration
> Of who I really am
> Your grace has made me stand
> Complete in you.

We are so grateful to the Lord for delivering us that we are now working with Reachout Trust to try to teach Christians how to reach these people.

Thirty-one Years A Jehovah's Witness

Jean Cleave

My earliest recollection of anything scriptural is being asked the question 'Who made you?'—the answer, of course, being, 'God'. Unfortunately I misunderstood and heard, 'Who made you God?' I always knew that I could talk to God, and said my prayers, and as a three-to-four-year-old I asked Him that question often.

My three sisters and I regularly attended Sunday school where, later, I became a teacher and was confirmed. When, at seventeen, I moved to another area to work and met Edward, my husband-to-be, I gradually drifted away from a place of worship and eventually stopped attending altogether. We did, however, decide on a church wedding, and our three children were christened and attended Sunday school. Our daughter joined the choir but refused to be confirmed for some reason unknown to me.

Death Opened the Door

Jehovah's Witnesses occasionally called, but I always told them that I was happy with the church, even though at the time I didn't go to one. However, when my father died in August 1957, I began to listen to them seriously for the first time. Five months later, my mother-in-law, who had lived with us for over sixteen years, also died. Grief-stricken, I then opened the door for the Jehovah's Witnesses to call and started regular studies with them. At first our youngest child, five at the time, left Sunday school and studied with me, but later, when he had to put more effort into his school work, he used this as an excuse to stop attending the Kingdom Hall.

My husband was against me associating with the Jehovah's Witnesses and we often quarrelled about the matter. I insisted, though, because he had no religion and only attended a place of worship for a wedding or funeral. On rare occasions he would allow me to use the car to go to meetings, sometimes I hitch-hiked, but more often I would borrow our son's cycle to go to the Kingdom Hall five miles away.

Jehovah's Test

Unknown to Ed, I was baptized on our wedding anniversary, 27th September 1959. With his antagonism, the annual Witness conventions were often a problem to get to, but I usually succeeded one way or another and felt Jehovah was testing my obedience to Him. After several years we became friendly with a couple of similar age, and Ed actually started having a weekly study where the question of baptism arose. I thought my prayers had been answered. It was not to be, though, and at this point Ed ended his studies.

Despite the disappointment, I continued to follow in the way of the Society, and even started on the door-to-door work. I did not always enjoy it, but I wanted to obey Jehovah and do His work. Looking back, I realize that I went out of duty, because my report had to be handed in at the end of each month, and not because of a calling from the heart. Every Jehovah's Witness is expected to do at least ten hours a month on the doors, otherwise it is considered unfair to the publishers who work hard, and failure to put in these hours also brings down the average hours of the congregation. I personally preferred 'incidental' witnessing and found this easier than going door to door.

When our son decided he wanted to go to college for further education I was very unhappy because the Watchtower advised it was better not to go as the 'time of the end' was so near. Fortunately, as it turned out, his dad had the last word and off he went to college. Now thirty-seven, nineteen years after Armageddon was supposed to come, he is a teacher, married with three children. When decisions such as this had to be made, I naturally would try to please Jehovah, but Ed told me that our married partnership was being marred by my determination to keep to the Watchtower teachings. As I was determined, I'm sorry to say our disagreements were frequent.

Problems

Life continued like this until 1988, when the problems which would lead to my leaving the Watchtower organization started. Although I did not know it then, I realize now that God was giving me a chance to find the 'real truth' that I had prayed so often for Ed to have.

The problems began while I was away nursing an aunt who was sick with cancer. Ed was suddenly taken ill; he was coping all right with my natural sister's help but as it was Easter he couldn't get any advice for the special diet he needed. My sister, who was a Jehovah's Witness, contacted the wife of an elder from the local Witness congregation who had suffered with the same complaint and would know what foods Ed could and couldn't eat. The elder's wife promised to see Ed, but she never even phoned or wrote, let alone visited. Ed's condition worsened, and I eventually managed to get my aunt into a home so that I could be with my husband who, by now, was having specialist treatment. I began to wonder where true Christian love was—it was certainly missing. Was it because I was unable to attend meetings more often? No one seemed to care.

After Auntie died, and Ed had improved, I started attending the meetings again in the Kingdom Hall, but the feeling was so different. Probably, I thought, it was the new bigger hall that made the difference. However, one Sunday morning the public talk seemed so uninteresting, and although I put my hand up to answer questions during the Watchtower study, no one seemed to notice me. I just felt 'flat'. I thought I must be a hypocrite and decided there and then to cancel my subscriptions to the *Watchtower* and *Awake!* magazines and finish completely with the Watchtower organization. When I got home and told Ed, he didn't believe that I had finished with the Witnesses, but I was beginning to see that love was missing.

Oxfam

For nearly twelve years I'd been a voluntary helper in the local Oxfam shop. The elders had often told me that it would be better if I went out on the door-to-door work. Jehovah would care for those in need in His own time but we needed to be out in our area. I would always feel guilty when a Jehovah's Witness entered the shop, but deep down I didn't really think I was doing wrong.

Anyway, one day soon after my decision to leave the Watchtower Society, a Witness came into the shop and I told her I felt spiritually low. I cried to her and she promised she would visit me. In actual fact, she sent another Witness along the next day who promised she would come back. Neither of them appeared again. However, shortly after, another couple called because they were on the doors in my area. They had a cup of tea but that was the last of their visits too. I now know it was a blessing they stayed away.

King's Coach

One evening, as I was leaving the Oxfam shop, I noticed a big coach on the Parade and decided that I would visit this 'King's Coach' on the following Saturday. I set off with my New World Translation and *Scriptures Inspired* book and spent more than an hour talking with members of the Christian team from the coach. I didn't use my books, in fact I didn't tell the team I was a Jehovah's Witness for quite a long time. When the conversation, which was very pleasant, came to an end I received an invitation to the evening meeting they were holding in the Upper School. I went home and suggested to Ed that we should go, and to my great surprise, because he liked his Saturday TV programmes so much, he agreed to come with me.

We arrived at the meeting a little late and sat in the seats nearest the back because I felt guilty being there. During the evening one speaker said, 'We had a Jehovah's Witness at the coach this morning who talked with us for a long time.' I nearly died of embarrassment because it was just as if they'd given out my name. On the way out we received an invitation to go to hear Peter Scothern the following week.

We promised my brother-in-law and his wife that we would go with them the following Friday, but we thought if we went on our own first, we would know what was what and not get pushed into anything. Wednesday evening therefore saw Ed and I arrive after the meeting had started, and again went to the back row feeling guilty. At the end of the meeting, when they started laying hands on people and some fell over, I was terribly scared and asked Ed if we could leave straight away. The Watchtower teach that such things are from evil spirits and I wanted to get out as soon as possible.

Ed said we would leave immediately it was finished, but on the way out he met an old school friend who explained the wonderful healings that had taken place. I still doubted that it was true, and questioned if it was scriptural, and behind everything that guilt feeling was still there.

Yet when Friday came, despite feeling guilty and having a good excuse not to go, because Ed was not well, I kept my promise to attend. I now know that the Lord was with us because just as I was about to leave the house, I saw an elder from the Witness congregation coming up the front path. Had he been a minute earlier I would not have had my coat on, and had he been five minutes later Ed would have been alone and probably invited him indoors. As it was he simply remarked, 'Oh, I see you're going out, I'll call again.'

Ask Jesus In

At the end of that Friday meeting I silently repeated the prayer to ask Jesus into my life; I even raised my hand when asked to do so; but when they invited us to go to the front, that was too much for me. My brother-in-law asked if I wanted to go out, to which I replied with an emphatic, 'No!' In a little while they started praying for the sick, and I started to cry because I so longed for Ed to get better. At this point a lady, a complete stranger, came across and tried to explain to me what was happening. I was still afraid because of the Watchtower teachings, but something seemed to say to me, 'What's here is love.' I gave in, and the lady and her friend walked with me to the front, as I cried and sobbed bitterly. I stood directly before my brother-in-law, who says seeing me give myself to the Lord made it one of the happiest days of his life.

Excited Then Deflated

I came home excited that I had accepted Jesus as my Saviour and because Ed had been prayed for. This happiness was soon to be shattered, though, when on the following Tuesday, two elders from the Watchtower Society called. Very quickly they reduced me to a wreck by the questions they fired at me: Why had I gone to those meetings? Had I prayed about it? Had I asked for forgiveness? Did I realize I was with the evil slave class, the Harlot, Babylon the Great? There were so many questions and cruel remarks that Ed left the room. I became very depressed for days and felt absolutely lost. I would phone my sister (not the one who was a Jehovah's Witness) and pour out my heart to her. She advised me to forget the Watchtower organization and tell them to stay away. When she would ask, 'Why are you crying?' all I seemed to be able to say was, 'I don't know.' 'What do you mean you don't know?' she would ask, only to receive the reply, 'I don't know what I don't know.' We can see the funny side of those conversations now but at the time I was in a bad state.

Ex-Jehovah's Witnesses

Somehow an ex-Jehovah's Witness, Philip Mawson from Truro, who had recently left the Society and become a Christian, heard about me and wrote to me offering to visit and loan me two videotapes: *Witnesses of Jehovah* and *How to witness to Jehovah Witnesses*. Both these videos were to show me the falseness of the Society and at the same time open my eyes to the truth. Philip came with three other ex-Jehovah Witnesses from Truro. It struck me that these people were prepared to travel miles to help me, whereas the Jehovah's Witnesses living on my doorstep deserted me and could only criticize. This was a big uplift to me. I thank God that Philip was led to me.

When the elders called again I had seen the videos and so was able to ask them some questions of my own. First, though, they asked me what I had been up to lately. To which I replied, 'Well, I haven't been to any more meetings.' Having asked Ed to stay with me, I had courage to ask them questions: Did they know that there had been a mansion built for Moses and other prophets to return to in the 1930s and that the Society sold it quietly in the early 1940s because they failed to appear? Yes, they understood this to be true. I then asked why the congregation wasn't told, and recalled the scripture that says, 'If God prophesies it is bound to come true; God cannot lie.' I went on to mention their many false dates, to which they replied, 'All religions make mistakes.'

I told them about things that had happened regarding our congregation which I personally felt were not right in Jehovah's eyes. One incident in particular was the time when a couple were not allowed to hold their wedding at the Kingdom Hall even though both were active Witnesses. The reason given for the refusal was that they were not quite 'normal', and if they had children it would be a bad witness to the world. I thought it was very unChristian to withhold Jehovah's blessing and to advise them to wait until Armageddon before getting married. I understand their wedding day was a happy occasion and they are a devoted couple. This and other incidents used to make me cringe during my time as a Witness, but the decisions of the elders are always taken as correct and scriptural.

Adultery Against Jehovah

During their interview I was informed that I had not been a Witness for a long time and I had become a non-reporter. I said, 'Jehovah knows what I have done' and quoted Ephesians 2:8–9 on being saved by grace through faith, only to be told, 'That's a grey area.' This is when my courage grew stronger and becoming hot under the collar I exclaimed, 'Why all this hassle? I haven't turned my back on the Bible. Anybody would think I had committed adultery or murder.' Their reply was probably the hardest knock I took in the whole episode: 'You have committed adultery against Jehovah and fornication with Satan.'

Amidst my tears I spoke about the Alpha and the Omega in Revelation 1:8 and 22:12–13, but was told that these scriptures were spurious. Ed then asked the elders to see the videos but of course they refused saying it was against the organization. Finally, they decided to leave telling me it was a pity I had not made up my mind which way I was going. I quickly pulled out a letter, addressed to the elders, from under a cushion and handed it to them. They obviously guessed I was leaving and so they warned me that by disassociating myself I would lose many friends because they would never speak to me again. I asked why this had to happen and was informed that it was possible I might encourage weak ones to leave by talking about the Trinity and other matters. The next day Ed phoned them and again asked them to see the videos, but again they refused. We've since purchased our own copies from Reachout Trust and many have borrowed them to see for themselves what the truth is.

New Church

Ed and I were approached by Pastor John Willoughby from the Assemblies of God church and we felt it was exactly what we wanted—a simple meeting in a hired hall without any crosses or other decorations. God knew where to lead us. We attend regularly for worship on Sundays and the Bible class on Thursdays. We both now take communion, knowing that it is not only for the 144,000 anointed ones, as the Watchtower teach. I renewed my vows on 29th January 1990 and was baptized on 29th April. Ed was baptized on 12th August.

Things are so different now. I used to call on one lady and offer to exchange *The Watchtower* for *Redemption* magazine and was annoyed when she refused, saying my organization was a cult. Now I am the *Redemption* secretary for our church. My prayers have also been answered for Ed because although he is still having specialist attention we know that it is divine healing that has prolonged his life.

The greatest thing, though, must be the new relationship Ed and I have—no longer apart in our thinking and no longer having to be secretive. We have been married almost fifty years and I can honestly say that the last year or so has been the happiest time of our marriage. Even our children say that we've altered and that we've now got smiling faces.

One Of The Great Crowd Of Jehovah's Witnesses

Robert Stewart

I was brought into the Jehovah's Witnesses as a child of four because my parents were interested in their beliefs, and so grew up with the Witnesses, not knowing anything different.

As a child I was always conscious of the fact that I was different—when children in the street had birthday parties or special celebrations I wasn't allowed to be with them on those days. And sometimes, when relatives who weren't Witnesses sent me presents, they would be returned, which to a child was a little confusing.

The Witnesses did try to compensate for this teaching about not celebrating birthdays, and in our local congregation they introduced what they called a 'happy day' which we celebrated instead of birthdays or Christmas. A day would be set aside especially for you, and that meant you could enjoy yourself without celebrating a pagan festival.

Make the Truth Your Own

This was life as I knew it, and I attended my first Jehovah's Witness Assembly in 1950. As I reached my late teenage years, though, I was encouraged by the elders to 'make the truth my own' instead of just being in the Witness organization because of my parents. I was encouraged to look into the Witness teaching myself, and I found that as I did, it seemed to raise more questions than it answered. I started to read the New Testament using the Watchtower Bible and discovered several areas which caused me concern and which I felt I would need to discuss with a mature Witness. However, I was still baptized into the organization in 1956.

For over ten years I pioneered with the Witnesses and worked an unassigned territory in the Highlands and Islands off the west coast of Scotland. I moved congregations three times, in response to the call to 'serve where the need is greatest'. I served as a ministerial servant and elder in the role of congregation book study conductor. I now look on these things as my vain works, in a similar way to Paul when he looked back:

> But whatever things were gain to me, those things I have counted as loss for the sake of Christ.... I have suffered the loss of all things, and count them but rubbish (Phil 3:7–9).

Doubts About the Society

I guess everyone in the organization had minor doubts from time to time. These were not doubts about the Scriptures, but about the Watchtower Society and their interpretation of Scripture. If you came across interpretations that caused you to doubt you were always encouraged to 'wait on Jehovah'. As we shared the things that puzzled us with the elders they would freely admit that they too were frankly puzzled about certain things, but told us we were to remain faithful to the organization and wait for the Governing Body to reveal these things in due time. We were always encouraged not to think ahead of what was printed in the magazines and books at the moment. If we did it was called presumptuousness, and this was a characteristic of Satan.

Private Groups

In my own circle of friends there were people who were very sincere in searching for truth and very sincere in their devotion to Jehovah, but occasionally they would have problems in fully complying with what the Watchtower Society said was the current view on a particular doctrine. Sometimes we would meet together in private groups. Later, this was frowned on because it caused some people to leave the Society. However, in those early days, when we met together quite innocently, we would discuss the various things that were a problem to us. But at the end of the day we would always put the problems in the back of our minds and think that perhaps in a month or a year we would have a new magazine on the subject. We used to feel that if it was a worldwide question then the Holy Spirit would prompt enough people to write to the Society for a ruling to be given, and this was how the 'new light' would come through.

A Major Problem

My first major problem, however, arose in 1980 when I began to be convinced that the 'great crowd', who were supposed to have only an earthly hope, were 'declared righteous', or as I would say today, justified by faith. I did a lot of research using the Society's books and found a great deal of material which referred to the 'great crowd' and members of the 'other sheep' as 'righteous'. The Witness doctrine is that only the anointed, the 144,000, are declared righteous (justified by faith). The rest of us, those of us who were taught that we were part of the 'great crowd', were not justified by faith. We had to survive the Battle of Armageddon; we didn't know how we were going to do that, but if we did we would live through the 1,000-year reign of Christ and only then would we be declared righteous. But this time the Watchtower phraseology took on a different meaning. It actually meant to be pronounced perfect. So there is no element of faith or grace for those of us who thought we were of the 'great crowd'.

This was a problem for me personally because as a teenager I had the temptations that are there as one comes into manhood. I was aware of sin in myself, aware of thoughts that pulled me towards sin, and I became quite fearful of Armageddon because I knew I was not fully faithful to God.

In this turmoil I typed out quotations from the Society and, alongside, quoted scriptures which seemed to contradict them, such as 'was not also Rahab the harlot declared righteous' (Jas 2:25, NWT). In all innocence I shared this material with mature brothers of the body of elders and asked for their comments. I was shocked and horrified by the response. All of a sudden my close friends changed overnight. What I had written in full childlike innocence was suddenly sinister. To cut a long story short, I was asked to resign as an elder and not to discuss the matter with anyone. I had seen my first glimpse of the iron hand hidden inside the velvet glove.

Fear of the Committee

One thing that had always frightened me—and now the threat appeared even closer—was that if you were overtaken in some sort of sin then you would be called before the judicial committee. This is a group of three elders who quiz you about your particular sin, and if they feel you aren't repentent then they can discipline you. This actually had the adverse affect of making you not wish to discuss your personal problems with your elder because you knew if you did confide in one that he would report back to the body who would then visit and interrogate you. With this background of fear and turmoil I would take refuge in reading the Scriptures. I used to love reading the Books of Romans and Galatians especially.

Grace

At the beginning I found it hard to understand the concept of grace, but gradually the Lord started to speak to me. I discovered things by just reading the Scriptures that I'd never been taught through any magazine or any book that the Watchtower Society had given me. I began to understand what grace really meant. The Witnesses have no concept of grace, in fact the word is not used in their translation of the Bible. But by just reading the Scriptures I began to understand grace and that by my faith in the Lord Jesus Christ I was saved from all sin; not just past but present and future; it had all been taken care of at Calvary. As a Witness I had been indoctrinated into thinking that all the churches which were outside the organization were being misled by Satan, so I had no interest in what they were teaching. I therefore thought that I was discovering something new—I was actually discovering new light ahead of *The Watchtower* magazine. I know it sounds crazy but this is how I felt. I started to think that if I just waited a little bit longer then *The Watchtower* would reveal this because I couldn't be the only one beginning to understand it!

Scriptures Alive

For the first time in my life the Scriptures started to come alive to me and fill me with wonder. It then struck me that perhaps it was only my own congregation that did not understand them, and so I wrote to the Society in London with the same information I had presented to my local elders. I received a two-page reply suggesting that the 'great crowd were declared righteous...to a degree but not like that of the anointed'. Having received this reply there seemed to be nothing more I could do, so I shelved this 'doubt', along with the others, and took some consolation from a later *Watchtower* which was to adjust their position on the matter.

In fact, the problem over justification by faith didn't lead me to leave the Society. The problem that did started with *The Watchtower* of 15th August 1980. This issue contained an article on the 'great crowd' and used the Greek word *naos*. In my own study I found the *naos* was the inner sanctuary of the Temple. From this it was so obvious to me that the 'great crowd' were in heaven, but the Society told me that they were in the courtyard of the Temple. Something was very wrong! (To see what Robert discovered as he compared the Bible with the Watchtower publication see the next chapter.)

Other matters continued to trouble me but I still had the feeling that Jehovah would put things right. Having family responsibilities I was unwilling to leave the organization. As the years went by, however, I could not help but share the truths I was forever finding in the Scriptures. I would share these truths with my wife, children and close friends and as a result I was called in to see the elders again and again. It then started to cause a problem in our home. My wife was fearful that I was being misled by Satan and this fear eventually led to a rift in our marriage. She thought I was possessed and this led to many arguments between us, which were brought to the attention of the elders. At this time I was more than ever convinced from the Scriptures that I was being taught false doctrine. I started to become more voluble because a strain was being put on my marriage, and it was then made plain to me that I would be disfellowshipped if I did not recant of my beliefs.

Disfellowshipped

I was finally disfellowshipped in March 1986. Just one month later my wife and children, who are still Jehovah's Witnesses today, were persuaded to leave me, it being reasoned that their spiritual life was in danger! I suppose, looking back, that this might have been an attempt to emotionally blackmail me to recant, but I had by then found my Lord and Saviour Jesus Christ. The Watchtower had nothing to offer me any more but deceit, lies and, of course, the carrot of my wife and family.

One of the most difficult things to try to explain to anyone else is what the act of disfellowshipping does for you. If you can imagine your closest friends, your wife and your children, your relatives, everyone you've ever loved, all dying instantly in a jet crash then you might just get an inkling of the devastation you feel. When you are disfellowshipped the loss is tremendous—you can no longer have any contact with those you love. In effect it is actually worse because with death you have to learn to cope with the fact that those you loved are gone but with disfellowshipping there is always that hankering and hope that something might happen to enable you to be reunited with your loved ones.

Grace Again

The three years after being disfellowshipped were my 'wilderness' period. I then returned to the quiet and isolated life of a west coast Scottish crofting community. I found myself attending the local Church of Scotland services and took great comfort to hear the name of 'Jehovah' used very frequently. Much to my surprise, I found a minister preaching 'grace', and for the first time I made the connection with what I had read for myself about 'undeserved kindness' and being 'declared righteous'. I then discovered the writings of Martin Luther and was encouraged to share his joy in finding 'grace'! Of particular help was his commentary on Galatians.

Only in the last year have I learnt about events in Brooklyn in 1980 when a number of the headquarters staff left or were disfellowshipped because of reading the same scriptures I read and learning about 'grace'. Encouraged by this I made efforts to contact an old 'pioneer friend' and share what I had found. Can you imagine my joy when I discovered he was also 'out' and, like me, had found Christ? He gave me a copy of *Crisis of Conscience* to read. This is the story of Ray Franz's personal struggle, and how he left the Witnesses after discovering many inside workings of the Society from his nine years on the Governing Body. My friend also advised me of many others who have escaped from the Watchtower.

Since then, I have started my own ministry to reach more Jehovah's Witnesses and, thank God, there are signs of some fruit. I find the most effective method is to present the pure gospel of the Scriptures contrasted with the Society's teaching.

In all my years as a Jehovah's Witness going from door to door I never ever once met a Christian who shared the love of the Lord Jesus Christ with me, and I think that's a shame. What Christians tend to do when they meet Witnesses is to either slam the door or shout at them or declare that they are false prophets. In reality, the best thing they can do is share the love of Jesus with them, to let it radiate from themselves. If a Christian can love a Jehovah's Witness he is half way to winning that Witness to Jesus.

Jehovah's Witnesses, Revelation And The Great Crowd

Robert Stewart

As Jesus Christ was preparing to go to the cross He encouraged His disciples with these words:

> In My Father's house are many dwelling places; if it were not so, I would have told you; for I go to prepare a place for you. And if I go and prepare a place for you, I will come again, and receive you to Myself; that where I am, there you may be also (Jn 14:2–3).

After His death, the resurrected Jesus instructed his followers:

> Go therefore and make disciples of all nations, baptizing them in the name of the Father and the Son and the Holy Spirit, teaching them to observe all that I commanded you; and lo, I am with you always, even to the end of the age (Mt 28:19–20).

In obedience to their risen Lord, those original Christians preached the gospel, or good news. The hope to all who believed was to be with Jesus, in His 'Father's house', and this hope was for 'all nations', that is, everyone, everywhere.

Paul included this 'hope of eternal life' as a primary

doctrine of the gospel (Tit 1:2). Peter talked of our inheritance in heaven (1 Pet 1:3). Early Christians could proclaim that their citizenship was in heaven and that they were partakers of a heavenly calling (Phil 3:20; Heb 3:1).

One Hope

The early church was a united Christian body with one hope, but this unity was soon under attack. In Ephesus Paul urged the Christians to keep the bond of peace (Eph 4:3–6). In Corinth false apostles were at work, out to draw Christians away from Christ (2 Cor 11:4,13–15). There was a similar problem in Galatia (Gal 1:6–9). Note well Paul's warning. No man was authorized to change that gospel—not even 'an angel from heaven'! The price to pay for preaching a 'different' gospel was eternal condemnation.

This one hope, this one gospel, has been the traditional teaching of the Christian church for almost 2,000 years. In our generation, however, there has arisen a 'different' gospel, a 'new' good news, a gospel other than the one which was preached by Paul and the early Christians. This 'good news' is preached by Jehovah's Witnesses and proclaims that millions of Christians have a hope of everlasting life on earth, not in heaven.

Judge Rutherford

The doctrine of an earthly 'hope' was first introduced by the president of the Watch Tower Bible and Tract Society, Joseph F. Rutherford, on Friday, 31st May 1935, to an audience of Jehovah's Witnesses in Washington, DC, America. It was published in a two-part article entitled 'The Great Multitude' in *The Watchtower*, 1st and 15th August of that same year.

The information presented was a change to the previous teachings of Jehovah's Witnesses. Their founding president, Charles T. Russell, had taught that the 'great crowd' had a heavenly hope. That was the accepted teaching for over fifty years. When Rutherford became the president of the Watch Tower Society in early 1917, at first he continued to preach a heavenly hope for the 'great crowd'. This new good news, therefore, was not just different to the ear of a Christian, it was also different for all Jehovah's Witnesses.

It is of interest that this doctrine of the 'great crowd' was the cause of many leaving the Society in the early 1980s. Following this the Society tried to repair the damage by publishing an article in *The Watchtower* of 15th August 1980, entitled, 'The "Great Crowd" Renders Sacred Service Where?' (hereafter referred to as the *article*). We will use this *article* as the basis for our examination of this teaching of the Society.

The 'Great Crowd': Scriptural Basis

The scriptural basis for discussion of the 'great crowd' is Revelation 7:9–17 (scripture quotations are taken from the New World Translation). We will use this to examine the biblical criteria to describe the location of the 'great crowd' and compare it with the Watchtower explanation.

This scripture tells us three things concerning the 'great crowd': first, they are before the throne of God (v 9); second, they render divine service to God (v 15); and third, they do this in God's sanctuary (v 15). Let us examine these expressions, in that order.

The 'Great Crowd': Before the Throne

This description is similar to that found in verse 9 where the 'great crowd' are 'standing before the throne and before the Lamb'. Where is the throne? Revelation tells us that it is God who is seated on the throne, and the apostle John confirms that the throne was set in heaven (Rev 4:2; 7:10; 19:4). We should remember, also, that John had responded, in his vision, to the invitation from heaven to 'come up here' and was ushered through the 'open door in heaven' to behold events disclosed there (Rev 4:1).

The expression 'before the throne' (Greek, *enopion tou thronou*) is unique to Revelation, where it occurs nine times. The Greek word *enopion* is formed from *en* which means 'in' and *ops* which means 'the eye'. *Enopion* refers, therefore, to that which is before or opposite a person, towards which he turns his eyes, that which is in one's sight or hearing or, metaphorically, in the mind's eye. Bible translators render *enopion* as 'before', 'in the sight of' and 'in the presence of'. The 'great crowd' are described, consequently, as being 'before the throne', 'in sight of the throne' or 'in the presence of the throne'.

Elsewhere in Revelation the seven lamps, the glassy sea, the golden altar, the seven spirits, the twenty-four elders, the angels, the four living creatures and the 144,000 are all said to be 'before the throne' (see 1:4; 4:5,6,10; 7:11; 8:3; 14:3). The Watchtower Society also say of these that they are before the literal throne in heaven.

Seven lamps and glassy sea

> Those seven symbolic lamps suggest that, in the fulfillment of John's vision, God is throning in his heavenly temple...the 'glassy sea like crystal' suggests purity, cleanness, on the part of those who approach God (*Then is Finished the Mystery of God*, p 14).

Golden altar

[The golden altar is where] their prayers through Christ needed to be acceptable just like sweet incense to God in his heavenly temple (*Ibid*, p 211).

Seven spirits

The 'seven spirits of God' are later pictured as eyes...possessed by...the Lord Jesus Christ, when he approaches God's throne and takes the scroll... (*Ibid*, p 155).

Twenty-four elders

The entire body of anointed Christians who, proving faithful till death, receive the promised reward of a heavenly resurrection and thrones near that of Jehovah (*Aid To Bible Understanding*, p 1251).

Four living creatures

In the vision the presence of the four living creatures together with the seven lamps of fire and the glassy sea like crystal *before God's throne* strongly suggests that the apostle John is seeing Jehovah God enthroned in his heavenly temple (*Then is Finished the Mystery of God*, p 20, emphasis added).

144,000

Where are these 144,000...standing with the Lamb...around the throne of Jehovah God in heaven (*Babylon the Great has Fallen*, p 461).

Summary of 'before the throne'

The phrase 'before the throne' is a unique description used by the apostle John, only in Revelation, and seven out of the nine times it appears Jehovah's Witnesses are convinced that it means being 'in the temple of God where is the heavenly throne'. The remaining two occurrences are found in Revelation chapter 7 verses 9 and 15 where the 'great crowd' are said not to be before God's throne.

The question must be asked, in view of the foregoing: when the apostle John saw the 'great crowd...standing before the throne', where did he see them? Did he see them in the Temple of God and in the presence of His heavenly throne or, as the Witnesses teach, did John describe them as being on earth? Which answer is consistent and harmonious with John's use of the expression 'before the throne'? Indeed, which answer is consistent with the Watchtower Society's own interpretation of the phrase?

The *article* does not go into the above detail. The argument presented is emotive and almost intimidatory. Paragraph 4 reasons:

> As regards those who today consider themselves part of the 'great crowd' that is now being formed, do they expect to go to heaven and become spirit creatures like angels? Do they even want to go to heaven? They will tell you, no! (pp 14–15).

What the article does not tell is that if a Jehovah's Witness who considers himself of the 'great crowd' was to declare a hope of going to heaven and share this with others, he would be brought before a judicial committee and risk being disfellowshipped. So much for the Watchtower explanation as to why 'before the throne' means on earth for the 'great crowd'. Elsewhere they reason:

Since they are standing before the throne of God and before the Lamb Jesus Christ, are they up in heaven? No! They are on earth and they will stay on earth.... In this age of radar and television we can appreciate how the Almighty God and his Lamb, Jesus Christ, can have before them this 'great crowd', even though here on earth (*Then is Finished the Mystery of God*, p 195).

We will leave you to decide if such an argument is reasonable and, more to the point, if such a conclusion is in harmony with the New Testament teaching that there is only 'one hope' for those who believe in Jesus Christ.

We now turn our attention to the second clue to the location of the 'great crowd' contained in Revelation 7:15.

The 'Great Crowd': Rendering Divine Service

This phrase is a translation of the Greek word *latreuo*, which is the verb form of the noun *latreia*. To understand what the apostle John saw the 'great crowd' doing, we need to see what he understood by these words.

In his letter to the Romans, Paul informs us that God's people, the Israelites, had been entrusted with the divine service (*latreia*) (Rom 9:4). The letter to the Hebrews tells us that only the priests could enter into the first Tabernacle to accomplish the divine service (*latreia*) (Heb 9:1–6). Christians are advised that those earthly regulations for divine service are only a shadow of the good things to come in heaven (Heb 8:5; 10:1).

The Reality

In the heavenly reality, Jesus, our great High Priest, has sat down at the right hand of the throne of the Majesty in heaven, and serves in the sanctuary (Heb 4:14; 8:1–2). By believing in Jesus Christ, by accepting His perfect sacrifice for our sins, we too can have confidence to enter this heavenly sanctuary (Heb 10:19). This is the 'one hope', the 'one faith' of all true Christians.

The apostle John was fully aware of the meaning of the Greek words *latreuo* and *latreia*. He would fully understand the spiritual truths found in the letter to the Hebrews, and so when he records that he saw the 'great crowd' rendering divine service in God's sanctuary, what reasonable conclusion can we come to? Did John see the 'great crowd' in the heavenly sanctuary or, as the Witnesses teach, did he describe them as being on earth?

The *article* goes into great detail about this sacred service.

> The 'great crowd' find themselves in the earthly courtyards of Jehovah's spiritual 'temple' and are seeking to render 'sacred service' fearlessly to the God of Abraham (p 23).

The *article* further explains that the sacred service includes obedience to God under persecution, preaching from door to door and making disciples. From this interpretation we can see that the Witnesses believe that Revelation 7:15 is a current event, happening now, and not a future occurrence. In fact, the *article* states that the 'great crowd' have been rendering sacred service on earth since 1935.

This final point leads us to a Watchtower contradiction. First we read:

> John sees here, not the gathering of the 'great crowd' in progress, but the completed picture, the fully gathered though un-numbered 'great crowd' (*Then is Finished the Mystery of God*, p 195).

The *article* however states:

Ever since this 'great crowd' began to be gathered in 1935 (p 21).

Which interpretation is correct, and which is in error? Or, in view of the letter to Hebrews, are both interpretations in error? All will become clear as we examine the third clue contained in Revelation 7:15.

The 'Great Crowd': In God's Sanctuary

With these words the apostle John, once and for all, demolishes all false teaching about the location of the 'great crowd'. A true understanding of this phrase was a key factor that led to vast numbers of Jehovah's Witnesses leaving the Society during the spring of 1980.

Some Bible translations read that the 'great crowd' are in God's sanctuary, others read that they are in God's Temple. Is this significant? Indeed it is, because the Watchtower Society base their whole argument on the meaning of the Greek words. For this reason we must establish exactly what is meant by these words. First, what would a Jew understand the sanctuary to be?

Moving the sanctuary

When the Israelites constructed the Tabernacle, instructions were given concerning its transportation, and an interesting distinction is drawn between that which constitutes 'the sanctuary' and that which constitutes 'the Tabernacle'. Numbers 4 gives us a list of items which constitute 'the sanctuary', as carried by the sons of Kohath, and from this list we discover that 'the sanctuary' was not so much the edifice or structure but, rather, the particular area set apart to hold the items sanctified to God. By contrast, Numbers 10 shows that the sons of Gershon and the sons of Merari transported 'the Tabernacle', the actual structure consisting of such items as the tent cloths, entrance screen, the hangings of the court-yard, and so on. From this information we clearly see that 'the sanctuary' was the part of the Tabernacle set apart for sacred and holy worship of God. The area was known as the Holy of Holies.

The Tabernacle continued to contain God's sanctuary until the reign of King David. David didn't feel right living in a grandiose house of cedars while the ark of the cov-enant, representing God's presence, remained in a tent. Thus David drew up plans for his son, Solomon, to build a house as a sanctuary (1 Chron 28:10). The sanctuary, therefore, became the central point of a whole Temple complex, the actual sanctuary building, containing the ark of the covenant, being known as 'the house of Jehovah' (2 Chron 3:1–3; 5:14; 7:2; 26:18–19).

The New Testament continues to show this distinction by the different Greek words used to describe 'the sanctu-ary' and the general Temple area as a whole. There are, in fact, three separate Greek words used in the New Testa-ment to describe the Temple. One of these words, *oikos* or *oikia*, simply denotes a house or a dwelling and is used to describe the house of God (eg Mt 12:4). Its meaning is not disputed so we will concentrate on the other two words which are subject to much controversy and conten-tion when it comes to their translation by the Watchtower Society.

Accurate translation

The correct translation of these two Greek words, *naos* and *hieron*, is vital to understanding the location of the 'great crowd' in Revelation. The Greek word *naos* occurs forty-six times in the New Testament, and a careful study of these occurrences proves how it should be translated. (See Appendix 1 at the end of this section for a full list.) For example, when Jesus died we read that 'the curtain of the sanctuary (*naos*) was rent in two' (Mk 15:38). Mark uses the word *naos* to define the sanctuary building.

Luke is also clear in his use of *naos*. Zechariah, the priest, entered into the sanctuary (*naos*) to offer incense on the altar. The fact that Luke limits the word *naos* to the sanctuary is evident from his comment that the people were 'praying outside at the hour of offering incense'. Although these people were in the Temple to pray, Luke clearly says they were outside the *naos*, whereas Zechariah was in the sanctuary (Lk 1:8–22).

That *naos* was the sanctuary of the inner Temple is confirmed by the Jewish historian of the first century, Flavius Josephus. Josephus was an actual eye witness of the Temple in Jerusalem and he corroborates the precise meaning of the *naos*. He provides a detailed description of the Temple, and after describing the outer cloisters of the Court of the Gentiles, he informs us that upon approaching the second court:

> There was a partition made of stone all round, whose height was three cubits: its construction was very elegant; upon it stood pillars, at equal distances from one another, declaring the law of purity, some in Greek, and some in Romans letters, that 'no foreigner should go within that sanctuary'; for that second temple was called 'the Sanctuary' [*ho naos*], and was ascended to by fourteen steps from the first court (*The Wars of the Jews*, Bk V, ch V, 2).

Sanctuary Evidence

Further confirmation can be found in various Greek lexicons and Bible dictionaries. For example:

> *naos*...the sanctuary in the Temple, into which only the priests could lawfully enter (W.E. Vine, *Expository Dictionary of New Testament Words*, p 1138).

> *naos*...the sacred building alone...only priests
> could enter the *naos* (*The Interpreter's Dictionary of
> the Bible*, Vol II, p 551).

> *naos* is from the root word *naio*, meaning to dwell,
> and thus the sanctuary was the house of God, the
> divine habitation (George V. Wigram, *The English-
> man's Greek Concordance*).

In view of this evidence, from the Bible and from
secular authorities, some Bible translations consistently
render the Greek word *naos* as 'sanctuary', eg, Robert
Young's Literal Translation of the Holy Bible. Indeed,
even the literal English of the Kingdom Interlinear Translation of the Greek Scriptures, published by the Watchtower Society, is consistent in always rendering *naos* as
divine habitation.

Regrettably, though, the New World Translation, published by the Watchtower Society, is not consistent on
translating *naos*. This is, however, going against •their
translation policy which we read of in the Introduction to
the 1984 revised edition:

> Uniformity of rendering has been maintained by
> assigning one meaning to each major word and by
> holding to that meaning as far as the context permits.

In reality, the New World Translation renders *naos*
four different ways: temple, temple (sanctuary), sanctuary, and shrine (see Appendix 1). Before we examine the
implications of this inconsistency we will look at the meaning of the other Greek word, *hieron*.

Hieron occurs seventy-one times in the New Testament
(see Appendix 2 for a complete list). It is generally translated as temple and sometimes as temple area, temple
courts, temple precincts, etc. For example, in John 10:23
the Colonnade of Solomon was in the *hieron*, as was the

Temple gate called Beautiful (Acts 3:2), and indeed so were the money-changers (Mt 21:12).

Josephus uses *hieron* to describe the whole Temple area, including the outer courts. W.E. Vine's *Expository Dictionary* defines *hieron* as 'distinct from the "*naos*", the inner sanctuary' (p 1138). Abingdon's *Interpreter's Dictionary* likewise says, under the heading, 'Temple':

> Two words are used in the Greek: '*naos*', meaning the sacred building alone, and '*hieron*', the whole sacred area, including various auxiliary courts, side chambers, and porticos. Both words are translated 'temple' (in the King James Version) without distinction, but the reader needs to keep the difference in mind, especially since only priests could enter the '*naos*' (Vol II, p 551).

Jesus is never spoken of as being in the *naos*, He is always in the *hieron*. The disciples are always found preaching in the *hieron*, never in the *naos*. These are vital clues. When John had his heavenly vision of the 'great crowd' he saw them rendering divine service to God in his sanctuary (*naos*)! Yes, the apostle John saw the 'great crowd' inside the holy dwelling of God, in the very centre of God's heavenly sanctuary. John did not see them in some external courtyard; they were not in a distant peripheral location, they were in the 'Father's house', just as Jesus had promised (Jn 14:2–3).

Naos

Naos occurs sixteen times in Revelation, but *hieron* is never mentioned. A good literal translation, therefore, would translate *naos* consistently as 'sanctuary' throughout, but the New World Translation is inconsistent when translating *naos*. In Revelation chapters 1 to 10 *naos* is rendered temple. In chapters 11 to 14, temple (sanctuary).

In chapters 15 to 20, sanctuary. Then in chapter 21 the meaning reverts to temple (see Appendix 1).

Because the New World Translation renders *hieron* as temple seventy-one times and *naos* as temple twenty-four times, the Jehovah's Witness is losing out on the fine shade of meaning which the distinctive Greek words convey. In fact, this regrettable situation is a contradiction to the Society's own stated policy in the Foreword to their translation, dated 9th February 1950, which reads:

> To each major word we have assigned one meaning and have held to that meaning as far as the context permitted. This, we know, has imposed a restriction upon our diction, but it makes for good cross-reference work and for reliable comparison of related texts or verses. At the same time, in order to bring out the richness and variety of the language of the inspired writers, we have avoided the rendering of two or more Greek words by the same English word, for this hides the distinction in shade of meaning between the several words thus rendered.

Earthly hope

With this in mind, we are now ready to approach the reasoning in the *article* which attempts to prove that the 'great crowd' are to receive an earthly 'hope'.

> The question revolves around that original Greek word that is variously translated as 'tent', 'temple' and 'sanctuary'. For example, in the Bible account of where Jesus Christ drove the money changers and merchantmen out of Herod's temple, the original Greek word used is '*naos*' (p 15).

It is true that the question of the location of the 'great crowd' does revolve around the meaning of *naos*, but it is false to say that Jesus drove the merchants from the *naos*. One Jehovah's Witness elder is reported to have described this statement as 'either an example of intellectual dishonesty or of intellectual ignorance' (Ray Franz, *Crisis of Conscience*, p 306). The false statement is repeated:

> It was from the courts of the outer temple (*naos*) that Jesus drove the money changers (p 15, summary box).

If we examine the four Gospel accounts of this incident (see Mt 21:12; Mk 11:15; Lk 19:45; Jn 2:14–15) we find that the actual Greek word used is *hieron*. In trying to prove that the Greek word *naos* could also include the outer courtyards of the Temple, the Watchtower have stooped to telling lies!

When Jesus, in John 2:19–21, was challenged by what authority He did these things, He replied, 'Destroy this sanctuary [*naos*], and in three days I will raise it up' Jesus, however, was not referring to Herod's Temple but 'the sanctuary [*naos*] that was his body'. The Jews, misunderstanding Jesus, challenged Him on His claim that He could rebuild the *naos* in three days. They exclaimed that it took forty-six years to build this *naos* in the first place. From this, the article tries to prove that *naos* included the outer courtyards of the Temple:

> By 'sanctuary', what did those Jews mean? Certainly not the inner sanctuary that contained the vestibule, the Holy and the Most Holy compartments. They meant the temple structure as a whole, including its courtyards, in one of which the money changers and merchantmen were doing business (p 15).

These are bold statements to make but, you will notice, no scriptures are produced to support this false claim!

Instead, the Watchtower attempt to build on their previous lie with authoritative and dogmatic bluster.

Forty-six years?

We need to establish that the inner sanctuary did take forty-six years to build because the Jehovah's Witness will argue that it took only eighteen months. This means that when the Jews said it took forty-six years to build the *naos*, they must have meant the whole Temple complex.

Josephus records that the original Temple, built by Solomon, was destroyed by King Nebuchadnezzar of Babylon (2 Chron 36:19). A new Temple was built that lasted until the time of King Herod the Great. He decided to rebuild the Temple, making it larger and higher (see *The Antiquities of the Jews*, XV, XI, 1).

Work began about 20 BC. The old building was pulled down, new foundations laid and the new Temple erected (see *ibid*, XV, XI, 3). The Temple itself was built by the priests in eighteen months, and Herod encompassed the entire Temple with large cloisters and outer enclosures which took eight years to build (see *ibid*, XV, XI, 5, 6).

We, of course, are now faced with a question. If it took only eighteen months to build the inner sanctuary (*naos*) and eight years to build the other courts and buildings (*hieron*), how could the Jews say to Jesus that the building work took forty-six years?

Three clear reasons

First, Herod's Temple was constantly being improved after its basic completion, and it was continually damaged through the struggles with the Romans. Also, defective foundations resulted in a partial collapse of the sanctuary.

Second, not only did work continue for forty-six years, but at the time the Jews made the comment to Jesus, Josephus records that there was still work to be completed on the sanctuary (*naos*). Indeed, when Jerusalem was besieged and the Temple destroyed by the Romans in AD 70, it still wasn't completely finished.

Third, Josephus gives accounts of many Jewish revolts resulting in Roman reprisals. On one occasion, 10,000 Jews went on the rampage in Jerusalem. They split into three groups, one of which took to the Temple. In consequence, the Romans set fire to the cloisters and destroyed them utterly (*Ibid*, XVII, X).

For these three reasons—general improvements, structural damage, and repeated war destruction—it is recorded that the original work-force of 10,000 was later increased to 18,000. It is only in AD 63, or thereabouts, that Josephus can say:

> And now it was that the temple [*hieron*] was finished (*Ibid*, XX, IX, 7).

However, a footnote adds:

> Of this finishing, not of the *Naos* or holy house, but of the *hieron*, or courts about it, called in general the temple.

Without doubt, when Jesus talked about pulling down the sanctuary (*naos*) and rebuilding it in three days, He would have been touching on a very sore point. The Jews would have been painfully aware of the ongoing problems of a defective sanctuary which, even after forty-six years, had not been perfectly finished.

The Watchtower Society do not publish all these facts and, as a consequence, are open to the accusation of being deceptive in suggesting that John 2:20 implies that the *naos* includes the outer courtyards. The Society's drawings and graphic descriptions of the Temple are based on the very works of Josephus we have quoted and they must, therefore, be fully aware of the true situation.

With this clear evidence to the contrary, both from the Bible and recognized authorities, why is the Watchtower Society so determined to prove that the *naos* is not the inner sanctuary of God, even stooping to the use of deception and lies?

Further deception

Indeed, the *article* contains further deception. Not only do the Society tell a lie about Jesus driving the money-changers out of the *naos* and use deception in implying that John 2:20 proves that the Jews used *naos* to describe the whole Temple structure. But in paragraph 5 they again employ dishonesty. They quote Isaiah 66:6 from the New English Bible:

> That roar from the city, that uproar in the temple, is the sound of the Lord dealing retribution to his foes (p 15).

They point out that the Greek Septuagint translation of this verse uses *naos* for temple, and then add this comment:

> Very plainly the temple, sanctuary, or '*naos*', does not mean just the inner sanctuary, but the entire temple with all its structures (p 15).

The Society imply that the uproar is the sound of those suffering retribution at the hand of God. The implication is that God's foes would not be causing uproar in the inner sanctuary, therefore *naos* must refer to the entire Temple area. The deception used here is staggering.

Young's Literal Translation of the Bible brings out the real meaning of the original Hebrew used in Isaiah 66:6:

> A voice of noise is from the city, a voice from the

temple, the voice of Jehovah, giving recompense to His enemies.

The uproar is not from God's foes but is the very voice of God! And where would God's voice come from in the Temple—from an outer courtyard? No! The voice of Jehovah would roar from His sanctuary, from the *naos*! Again we see the desperate tactics of the Society to twist the true meaning of the Word of God.

In paragraph 6 the Society introduce the text of when Jesus was on trial before the Sanhedrin. Several testified that Jesus had said He would destroy the man-made Temple (*naos*) and in three days build another not made with hands (Mk 14:58). They then make the point that the entire Temple was destroyed in AD 70, not just the inner sanctuary, the implication being that Jesus foretold the destruction of the *naos* and the fulfilment included the destruction of the outer courtyards. This again is trickery!

The testimony given in Mark 14:58 is actually that of 'false witness' (v 57), and anyway does not refer to Jesus' prophecy regarding the coming destruction of the Temple. That prophecy is recorded in John 2:19–21 where, as we have already seen, Jesus was talking about His own death and resurrection. On the other hand, when we look at prophecies regarding the destruction of the Temple (see Mt 24:1–2; Mk 13:1–2; Lk 21:5–6; 19:44), Jesus never uses the word *naos* but *hieron*. It is quite remarkable that the Society use the word of a 'false witness' to seek to prove that Jesus used *naos* to describe the entire Temple area.

Finally, in paragraph 7, the Society quote Matthew 27:5:

Judas threw the money into the sanctuary (*naos*) and left them; then he went off and hanged himself (p 16).

They summarize this incident as follows:

> It was in the outer temple [*naos*] that Judas threw back the 30 pieces of silver (p 15).

No evidence is given, no reasoning is used. All they do is point out that some translations use Temple instead of sanctuary, therefore *naos* means the Temple with all its courts. But is it reasonable to conclude that Judas would throw the silver coins into the outer court? Remember, Judas received the money from the chief priests of the Temple, as the price to betray Jesus (Mt 26:15). The exclusive domain of the priests, in the Temple, was the sanctuary, the *naos*.

When Judas felt remorse and attempted to return the money, the chief priests would not take it from him and, therefore, Judas 'threw the money into the sanctuary [*naos*]'! (Mt 27:3–5). We must remember that Judas was trying to return the money to its source and, when frustrated by the priests' refusal, it would be only natural for Judas to throw it into the exclusive domain of the priests, into the *naos*. Why the Watchtower Society should find this unreasonable and conclude that Judas had to throw the money into some outer area of the Temple, where anyone, Jew or Gentile, could pick it up, is confusing and not supported by Scripture.

'Naos' on earth

The Watchtower Society, feeling they have provided proof that the *naos* included the outer courts, concludes with these words:

> Thus the 'great crowd' may be said to be in the 'temple' or '*naos*', of God and yet not be in heaven (p 16).

With this statement, the Society double their error. It is bad enough to suggest that the 'great crowd' are not in the *naos*, without twisting the Word of God further. They teach that the *naos* in which the 'great crowd' serve is on earth. Does this agree with what John says in Revelation? No! John talks of the sanctuary (*naos*) of God in heaven (see Rev 11:19; 14:17). Throughout Revelation it is clear that the sanctuary is a heavenly one; there is not a hint that the *naos*, or any part of it, is on earth. Regarding the use of the Greek word *naos* in Revelation, even the Society's Bible encyclopedia says:

> God's dwelling place in the heavens is a sanctuary, or a holy place. It is in this heavenly sanctuary that the apostle John, in vision, saw the ark of the covenant (*Insight on the Scriptures*, Vol 2, p 860).

It is in this heavenly sanctuary that John saw the 'great crowd'! In another book, the Society define this heavenly *naos* in these words:

> The temple sanctuary of God that was opened to John's view [in the Revelation] is the exclusive holy area of the heaven of the heavens where Jehovah sits enthroned (*Then is Finished the Mystery of God*, p 296).

Yes, it is in this holy area of the heaven that John saw the 'great crowd'!

In defiance of Scripture and in contradiction of their own definition of the heavenly *naos*, the *article* publishes a diagram (p 17) depicting the 'great crowd' in the outer Court of the Gentiles, otherwise known as the Courtyard of the Nations. Yet Revelation clearly says that the court-yard is outside the sanctuary (*naos*) (Rev 11:2). It is therefore impossible for the 'great crowd' to be in the courtyard when, as we have seen, they are in the *naos*.

Jehovah's Witnesses speak of the 144,000 (Rev 7:4; 14:1) as 'spiritual Israel'. According to Witness teaching, the 144,000 are an exclusive group of Christians who, alone, have a heavenly hope. By contrast, according to Witness teaching, the 'great crowd' are a secondary group of millions of Christians who have an earthly hope. If the heavenly group are called 'spiritual Israel', what do the Witnesses call the earthly group?

In various publications, the Watchtower Society refer to them as a 'mixed company', 'a group of aliens', 'foreigners' and 'non-Israelites' who associated themselves with the literal Israel to obtain benefits. The Society teach that these foreigners are a picture, or shadow, of the 'great crowd'. By depicting the 'great crowd' in the Courtyard of the Nations or the Court of the Gentiles, the Society are, in effect, calling the 'great crowd' an alien group of spiritual Gentiles!

Literal Israel looked down on the Gentiles as second-class citizens, inferior beings who had to be kept at a distance from themselves and, indeed, from God. A barrier was erected in the Temple to prevent these 'aliens', these foreign Gentiles, from getting anywhere near the holy sanctuary.

Speaking of this barrier, the apostle Paul explains in Ephesians 2:11–22 that the Gentiles used to be kept separate from God and excluded from the promises:

> But now in Christ Jesus you who formerly were far off have been brought near by the blood of Christ. For He Himself is our peace, who made both groups into one, and broke down the barrier, of the dividing wall...that in Himself He might make the two into one new man...so then you [Gentiles] are no longer strangers and aliens, but you are fellow-citizens with

the saints and are of God's household, having been built upon the foundation of the apostles and prophets, Christ Jesus Himself being the corner stone, in whom the whole building, being fitted together is growing into a holy temple [*naos*] in the Lord, in whom you also are being built together into a dwelling of God in the Spirit.

Paul's letters in the New Testament are full of his efforts to prevent 'false apostles' re-erecting the barrier that Christ had destroyed. However, in their doctrine of the 'great crowd', Jehovah's Witnesses are seen to be re-erecting the barrier between 'spiritual Israel' and 'spiritual Gentiles'. This is in defiance of the gospel that Paul preached:

> That through the gospel the Gentiles are heirs together with Israel, members together of one body, and sharers together in the promise in Christ Jesus (Eph 3:6).

What promise was that? The promise that Jesus gave to his followers:

> There are many rooms in my Father's house; otherwise, I would have told you. I am going there to prepare a place for you. And if I go and prepare a place for you, I will come back and take you to be with me that you also may be where I am (Jn 14:2–3).

In Revelation, Jesus gave John a vision of His Father's house, His heavenly sanctuary. In order to confirm the gospel that was being preached, Jesus showed John

A great crowd, which no man was able to number,

out of all nations and tribes and peoples and tongues, standing before the throne and before the Lamb...before the throne of God and are rendering divine service unto him day and night in his sanctuary (Rev 7:9–17).

Christians today, must stand firm in this 'one hope' for all those who believe in Christ and be ready to defend the good news against 'false apostles' who attempt to distort the gospel.

Appendix 1

The following is a list of the forty-six places where the Greek word *naos* occurs in the New Testament, together with the English equivalent as rendered by the New World Translation of Jehovah's Witnesses:

Matthew 23:16 temple
Matthew 23:16 temple
Matthew 23:17 temple
Matthew 23:21 temple
Matthew 23:35 sanctuary
Matthew 26:61 temple
Matthew 27:5 temple
Matthew 27:40 temple
Matthew 27:51 sanctuary
Mark 14:58 temple
Mark 15:29 temple
Mark 15:38 sanctuary
Luke 1:9 sanctuary
Luke 1:21 sanctuary
Luke 1:22 sanctuary
Luke 23:45 sanctuary
John 2:19 temple
John 2:20 temple
John 2:21 temple
Acts 7:48 houses
Acts 17:24 temples
Acts 19:24 shrines

1 Corinthians 3:16 temple
1 Corinthians 3:17 temple
1 Corinthians 3:17 temple
1 Corinthians 6:19 temple
2 Corinthians 6:16 temple
2 Corinthians 6:16 temple
Ephesians 2:21 temple
2 Thessalonians 2:4 temple
Revelation 3:12 temple
Revelation 7:15 temple
Revelation 11:1 temple (sanctuary)
Revelation 11:2 temple (sanctuary)
Revelation 11:19 temple (sanctuary)
Revelation 11:19 temple (sanctuary)
Revelation 14:15 temple (sanctuary)
Revelation 14:17 temple (sanctuary)
Revelation 15:5 sanctuary
Revelation 15:6 sanctuary
Revelation 15:8 sanctuary
Revelation 15:8 sanctuary
Revelation 16:1 sanctuary
Revelation 16:17 sanctuary
Revelation 21:22 temple
Revelation 21:22 temple

Appendix 2

The following is a list of the seventy-one places where the Greek word *hieron* occurs in the New Testament, always rendered into English as temple by the New World Translation:

Matthew	4:5; 12:5,6; 21:12(x2),14,15,23; 24:1(x2); 26:55.
Mark	11:11,15(x2),16,27; 12:35; 13:1,3; 14:49
Luke	2:27,37,46;4:9;18:10;19:45,47;20:1;21:5,37,38; 22:52,53; 24:53.
John	2:14,15; 5:14; 7:14,28; 8:2,20, 59; 10:23; 11:56; 18:20.
Acts	2:46;3:1,2(x2),3,8,10;4:1;20,21,24,25,42;19:27; 21:26,27,28,29,30; 22:17; 24:6,12,18; 25:8; 26:21.
1 Corinthians	9:13.

Winning And Keeping The Cultist For Christ

Doug Harris

This section contains a few brief comments on how to win Jehovah's Witnesses and Mormons to Christ. We are dealing here with our basic attitudes, not necessarily specific help with what to say, but this information can be obtained from Reachout Trust. See the advertisement pages at the back of the book for an idea of the type of help you can receive, or write to Reachout Trust for a full resource list.

Please read James 1:19—2:9 before continuing to read this section.

Accept Them As They Are

This attitude is a basic requirement and as such it must be of prime importance. We cannot start by telling the cults how wrong they are and list all the bad things they do. All that does is erect a brick wall between you and them and distances them, whereas you want to draw them to yourself and win them. The cult members believe they are right. They will have found the answer to some of their needs within the cult. In order to change they need to see an alternative that is attractive. This means that our life is as important as our word. This is especially true when we live with or work with the cult member or have regular contact with him or her.

Although we might not say these exact words to the cultists at the door, our attitude should be summed up as follows: I do not agree with all that you believe but I accept that you are genuine and sincere. If this is our heart attitude it will lead us to build a bridge of love to them that will not just demand that 'I must be right!' but will listen to what they believe and then share the true gospel in a humble and relevant way.

The more I'm involved in the cult work the more I realize the need for Christians to use 'apologetics'. The *Concise Oxford Dictionary's* definition of apologetics is 'reasoned defence', so by using apologetics we are not apologizing for being a Christian but finding analogies and illustrations that convey to people why becoming a Christian is a sensible and rational decision when all the facts are examined. Presenting the claims of Jesus using these bridge-building tactics usually allows us a fair hearing, thus giving the Holy Spirit the opportunity to do His job. Our job is to relate to the cult member and share the truth; the Holy Spirit's job is to convict of sin and lead him to salvation.

Jesus Our Great Example

Probably the best example of witnessing in a humble and relevant way is found in John 4 where Jesus meets the woman at the well. Let's just draw out a few points from this to encourage us to share lovingly as Jesus did.

Verse 6: Jesus is the true Servant. He knew what His calling was and was ready to share at all times. At this point He was tired and weary and could have been excused not bothering with this woman.

Verse 7: Whereas we might seek to make up an excuse not to talk to the cultist at the door, Jesus had genuine reasons, not excuses, why He should not talk. His best reason would have been that Jews had no dealings with

Samaritans. However, He did not allow hatred of a certain people or the social barriers of the day to stop Him reaching out to this lost person. Neither should we allow them, in our day, to stop us witnessing to the cultist. Some would tell us to leave them alone, but Jesus loved them enough to die for them, so whom am I to forbid them to hear the truth?

Please note that Jesus didn't immediately say, 'You adulteress, you'd better repent before it's too late!' He asks for a drink and at once opens Himself up to the woman, and because the woman is not threatened she opens up to Him. This is the way we need to relate— lovingly and genuinely opening up to people.

Verses 10ff: Jesus makes a very interesting statement that leads to a religious discussion. Jesus was content to go along this line to continue to build a bridge. He didn't mind taking time to relate to the woman, and after five minutes He didn't get tired and exclaim, 'You adulteress, stop trying to avoid the point, repent!'

Verses 16 to 18: Having finished the discussion, does Jesus now say, 'You adulteress....'? No! Jesus had clear knowledge about this woman via the Holy Spirit. Often the Holy Spirit will either put some information about the person we are talking to into our hearts or will cause us to talk about a subject that goes right to the heart of the cultist's need. Please note though how Jesus used the information in love. It was almost as if He said, 'We're having a great conversation here, why not call your husband so he can join us too.'

Verses 19ff: Jesus is prepared to talk to the woman on her level with her understanding rather than try to force His perfect knowledge on to her.

Verse 29: Please note the reaction of this woman to Jesus' revelation. It was not, 'What a rotten man. He's just insulted me', but 'Come and see a man who's told me all about my life. Could this be the Messiah?' As we open up our lives and allow the life of Christ to shine out of us I believe we will have something of the same reaction. It will not mean that every Jehovah's Witness or Mormon on our doorstep will be saved but they will go away with a big question mark in their lives: 'Could this be true?' We are to love them not judge them. We don't know why they came to be in a cult and it's not up to us to condemn them for maybe honestly seeking for God, but it is up to us to show them by love the way out of the cults.

Understand and Sympathize

We should never try to apply standards to others that we wouldn't put on ourselves or that God doesn't place on us. God did not give us a complete checklist before He poured out His grace on us. He saw there was repentance in our hearts and responded to our small move towards Him without our having reached the state of perfection. Cultists may have a number of problems in their lives and take a while to sort them out, but if they have made a genuine act of repentance to Christ He will meet them.

Hebrews 4:14—15:8 tells us of our great High Priest who sympathizes with our weaknesses. This doesn't mean that He condones sin in our lives but He does accept us as we are at His throne of grace. There we can find the help we need. We need to learn through the Holy Spirit to bring the cultists to that same High Priest and to that same throne where they can be sympathized with. The key to our sharing should of course be truth, but shared gently, not with an iron fist.

Do learn to understand the problems the cultists have. Maybe they will have to leave their family behind. Not only do we need to treat these difficult steps they must take with much love, we must also be prepared to give such people a new home. In other words, it's not just a matter of saying, 'Be blessed and may the Lord help you, goodbye.' It's telling them that any time they need it there is a place for them in your home.

Please also remember that many will find entering a church building for the first time a real problem. Many have been known to at least feel, if not actually be, physically sick when they enter what they have been told is 'Satan's kingdom'. Make it as easy as possible for them by maybe bringing them to a home group first, and then meet them outside the church building and walk in and sit with them the first time they come. Never put pressure on them to join the church either. Everything will be sorted out in time by the Holy Spirit. Remember they have just left an organization that they believed to be the only true church. If we put pressure on them to join another 'organization' soon after leaving the false one, we are giving them problems that they need not have.

Time and Patience

These two things may be lacking in our lives, but how we need to seek God's Holy Spirit to help us spend as much time with cultists as is necessary and also be very patient. Possibly they will just need friendship at some point; not every meeting needs to be 'spiritual'. Most will need vast amounts of love and care. Just as Jesus showed compassion and restored Peter in John 21, so we need to show that sort of care to the cultists.

There will be a time when Bible study is vital but please remember you can probably give out far more at one session than they can take in. Be sensitive and encourage them not just to substitute your teaching for the teaching the Society used to give them. They need to begin to develop their own relationship with God and everything we do should help them along that line. Remind them that they must go back to the Scriptures themselves and ask the Holy Spirit to lead them into all truth. Ideally, what we share should either give them guidelines as to where to look in the future or confirm and develop what God has already been saying to them.

Deliverance

All those who have been in the cults have been affected by the satanic realm in one form or another. I believe it is necessary for all to confess that the system they have been in is satanic, to repent of it, and declare to God, the principalities and powers of the air, and any watching on earth, that they want nothing more to do with it. Please note it is the system they need to accept as satanic, *not* the people. Once they have confessed and turned their back on it, you can pray a strong prayer in the name of the Lord cutting them off from the past and closing the doorway that Satan had into their life.

At the same time seek the Holy Spirit to fill the 'gap' that is left. This is the beginning of the work, but please remember that Jesus promised the Holy Spirit would lead into all truth. Seeking the Holy Spirit to fill their life and lead them from now on will set them on the road for growing in the truth and grace of God.

Spiritual Weapons for a Spiritual Battle

We are not battling against the people who are in the cults but against Satan and his armies who have blinded their eyes. Do remember therefore that we are to engage in the spiritual warfare of prayer to see these captives released. It is very helpful to be able to share the errors of the group they have been in and then the true gospel. But if this is not done with the enabling of the Holy Spirit little will result. Pray in specific ways for cult members, by name if you know them, in your home groups, families and church prayer meetings. Pray they will visit Christians in your area and pray the Christians will speak to them. God has made it clear in the Bible that such prayer gives Him the opportunity to move in an individual's life, and that in the end is what we are looking for.

If after all this you feel inadequate, please read the story of Gideon (Judg 6:1ff) and be encouraged at how God can use inadequates. He doesn't want us to feel important and powerful and boast of our persuasive arguments because then we are not relying on Him very much. However, He can use mightily someone who is nervous and shy but willing to trust Him.

> Not that we are adequate in ourselves to consider anything as coming from ourselves, but our adequacy is from God, who has also made us adequate as servants of a new covenant, not of the letter, but of the Spirit; for the letter kills, but the Spirit gives life (2 Cor 3:5–6).

Glossary of Jehovah's Witness Terms

Anointed The small select band of 144,000 Jehovah's Witnesses who alone will have a heavenly reward.

Apostates See *Evil Slave Class*.

Awake! This is one of the 32-page magazines (see also *The Watchtower*) that come out twice a month. It is similar to a 'spiritual Reader's Digest'.

Babylon the Great This biblical phrase is used to describe the whole of Christendom, ie, all churches except Jehovah's Witnesses are considered to be serving Satan and not Jehovah God.

Brooklyn The area of New York that houses the headquarters of Jehovah's Witnesses. When used it is usually interchangeable with either the 'Governing Body' or the 'Watchtower Society'.

Congregation Book Study Conductor The person appointed by the Jehovah's Witness congregation to lead a home book study.

Evil Slave Class Used especially to describe all those who were once Jehovah's Witnesses but have now turned their back on the organization. The term is sometimes extended to include any who speak against the Society whether they have been Witnesses or not. Active Jehovah's Witnesses are not allowed to speak to such people under the threat of disfellowshipping, ie, being thrown out of the organization.

Governing Body The group of men who live in Brooklyn, New York, and lead the Watchtower Society of Jehovah's Witnesses.

Great Crowd   All Jehovah's Witnesses, apart from the anointed. The great crowd have only an earthly inheritance and never expect to see the Father or Jesus face to face.

Harlot   Used similarly to *Babylon the Great*.

Increased Light   Whenever a change in doctrine or prophecy takes place it is said to come as a result of increased light. The term comes from twisting the meaning of Proverbs 4:18.

In the Truth   All Witnesses refer to themselves as being in the truth because they belong to God's sole organization.

Judicial Committee   The group of men from a congregation who will sit and judge whether an individual Witness should be reprimanded or even disfellowshipped for his conduct. Offences that can lead to Witnesses being called before the committee can range from smoking to committing adultery and from sharing Bible truth with other Witnesses to child beating.

Kingdom Interlinear Translation (KIT)   This translation contains the Greek text of Westcott and Hort, with a literal English translation on one side of the page and the New World Translation on the other. Witnesses are told they can check the truth of the original Greek Scriptures with this publication.

Ministerial Servant   Somebody who serves in an area of practical responsibility in a congregation of Jehovah's Witnesses.

New World Translation (NWT)   The version of the Bible translated by the Watchtower Society. Many scriptures, especially those dealing with the deity of Christ, have been altered to affect their teaching, but the Jehovah's Witness believes it is the most accurate of all Bibles.

Organization   The Watchtower Society of Jehovah's Witnesses.

Other Sheep   Alternative term to *Great Crowd*.

Pioneer   Someone who gives a specific number of hours a month to the door-to-door ministry. The time given ranges from 60 to 135 or so hours a month depending on the type of pioneer.

Pioneers usually need to have a part-time or early morning job to keep their family above the breadline while they spend so much time on the doors.

Public Talk   A meeting on a Sunday where an official of the Society gives a talk from an outline provided by the Society.

Publisher   Every Witness is called a publisher because he should be publishing the good news from door to door.

Theocratic   Literally meaning God's rule. Therefore the Watchtower Society are called a theocratic organization because they are the only one ruled by God.

Time of End   The period between 1914, when Jesus took His throne invisibly in the heavens, and the Battle of Armageddon, the battle that will destroy all the wicked and make way for the paradise earth.

Unassigned Territory   A part of a country that has not been given to a specific congregation of Jehovah's Witnesses to call on regularly in the door-to-door ministry.

The Watchtower   This is one of the 32-page magazines (see also *Awake!*) that come out twice a month. This is the main regular teaching vehicle of the Watchtower Society.

Watchtower Study   A Sunday meeting at which a particular article is read from *The Watchtower*. Questions are asked and answered from the text alone. Many Witnesses take time preparing for this meeting during the week.

Glossary of Mormon Terms

Baptism for Dead Mormons trace their genealogy and send names of their dead ancestors to the headquarters in Utah. Someone is then asked to be baptized on behalf of that person. Mormons believe that unless someone is baptized into the Mormon Church, even the dead, he will have no hope of entering the highest heaven in his future life.

Book of Mormon One of the Scriptures of the Mormon Church. It contains the supposed translation of the golden plates that Joseph Smith found. It is an account of God's dealings with those who lived in the Americas between 2247 BC and AD 421. It is also believed to contain the fullness of the everlasting gospel.

Doctrine and Covenants Another of the Scriptures of the Mormon Church. It contains revelations from God given to Joseph Smith and others.

First Presidency The leading authority group within the Mormon Church, consisting of three men, the first president and his two counsellors.

Pearl of Great Price The third set of Scriptures of the Mormon Church containing a selection of various writings of Joseph Smith and also translations of other ancient books.

The Prophet There is always one man who is designated the living prophet. What he says is taken as 'scripture' by a Mormon. If the living prophet says something that contradicts a prophet from the past then the living one has the most up to date revelation.

Salt Lake City   The town in Utah, America, that the early Mormons built and that is now the worldwide headquarters of the Mormon Church.

Temple Recommend   A piece of paper that it is necessary to have to be able to go through the secret temple ceremonies of the Mormon Church. To get it you must prove yourself 'worthy' to two Mormon officials. Being worthy includes paying your full tithe and keeping all Mormon commandments.

Twelve Apostles   Another leadership group in the Mormon hierarchy, beneath the first presidency.

Utah   See *Salt Lake City*.

AWAKE! TO THE WATCHTOWER

Doug Harris

A 256-page well documented book that gives great background understanding of the Jehovah's Witnesses and at the same time shows clearly how you can share the real Jesus with them.

In particular, it shows how the Watchtower Society constantly misquote well known scholars to try to prove that what the organization teaches is right.

If you want an in-depth look at Jehovah's Witnesses then this is the book for you.

For price and availability contact:

ALPHA PLACE, GARTH ROAD, MORDEN, SURREY
SM4 4LX
081-337 9716

THE TRUTH REVEALED

Bill Browning

This booklet is for use when the Jehovah's Witness first comes to the door. It contains many photostat copies of the Watchtower's own literature and shows where they have deceived their followers and used some very questionable versions of the Bible to support their own New World Translation.

At the back there are also scriptures to help deal with some of those difficult questions raised at the door.

For price and availability contact:

ALPHA PLACE, GARTH ROAD, MORDEN, SURREY
SM4 4LX
081-337 9716

AN ALTERNATIVE VIEW

Bill Browning

This publication is for follow-up work with a Jehovah's Witness. In an attractive folder giving helpful tips on how to talk to the Witness you will find 14 sheets on various tricky subjects that the Witness might throw at you, including the Trinity, blood and the 144,000.

Each sheet first gives a brief outline of what the Witness believes and then shows which scriptures you can use to share the real meaning of the Bible. We call the publication *An Alternative View* so that you can avoid a head-on collision, and the 'You're wrong!' approach, and instead say, 'Have you ever thought that there's another way of looking at that?'

For price and availability contact:

ALPHA PLACE, GARTH ROAD, MORDEN, SURREY
SM4 4LX
081-337 9716

CRISIS OF CONSCIENCE

Ray Franz

Ray is the nephew of Freddy Franz who, though quite old, is still president of the Watchtower Society. Ray was a member of the Governing Body for nine years and so is able to give interesting and helpful insights into the working of the Society.

The story is that of Ray's struggle to reconcile the way the Society was being run with truth. Finally he felt compelled to leave and give every Jehovah's Witness the opportunity to check the facts that brought him to his decision. Compulsive reading.

For price and availability contact:

ALPHA PLACE, GARTH ROAD, MORDEN, SURREY
SM4 4LX
081-337 9716

WITNESSES OF JEHOVAH

This 56-minute documentary-styled video first examines the background and history of Jehovah's Witnesses.

Then, through the eyes of ex-Witnesses such as Ray Franz, it helps you become aware of what you can share with the next Jehovah's Witness that calls at your door and the way to say it.

This video is ideal for use in all churches, and especially for small groups. You can even invite your neighbours to come and see it because not only does it give a clear warning about the Watchtower Society, it shows the lives of those who have been set free and have come to know Jesus Christ as their Saviour.

For price and availability contact:

ALPHA PLACE, GARTH ROAD, MORDEN, SURREY
SM4 4LX
081-337 9716

BEHIND THE VEIL

Doug Harris

This is the equivalent for Mormons to *The Truth Revealed*. It shows the mistakes and cover-ups from the past through the pages of the Mormons' own literature. It will help you sow doubt in the mind of the Mormon as to whether his church is really the only true one.

The final pages are dedicated to a presentation of how to share the real Jesus with a Mormon in a relevant way.

For price and availability contact:

ALPHA PLACE, GARTH ROAD, MORDEN, SURREY
SM4 4LX
081-337 9716

CHANGING WORLD OF MORMONISM

J. & S. Tanner

This book contains over 600 pages giving an in-depth look at Mormons. The Tanners come from Mormon families and have probably done more research into Mormonism than anyone else.

If you want to have a good understanding of Mormonism—this is the book for you.

For price and availability contact:

ALPHA PLACE, GARTH ROAD, MORDEN, SURREY
SM4 4LX
081-337 9716

Reachout has a great selection of books, cassettes and videos on Witnesses, Mormons and many other groups. You can also obtain a selection of tracts that can be used for giving to the Witness or Mormon or warning your neighbourhood of the dangers.

For our full resource list that covers cults, occult and New Age, write to:

ALPHA PLACE, GARTH ROAD, MORDEN, SURREY SM4 4LX
081-337 9716